Revolution Embassy LLC
CONFRONT THE SILENCE
www.revolutionembassy.org

MEDITATION & PRAYER YDS

To Lauren,
Be the Warrior God made you
to be; Shine your light for
all to see.

Matt Siler

MEDITATION & PRAYER YDS

PRAYER IS TALKING TO GOD.
MEDITATION IS LISTENING TO GOD. ™

YVETTE SILVA

BALBOA.
PRESS
A DIVISION OF HAY HOUSE

Balboa Press books may be ordered through booksellers or by contacting:

Balboa Press
A Division of Hay House
1663 Liberty Drive
Bloomington, IN 47403
www.balboapress.com
1-(877) 407-4847

Because of the dynamic nature of the Internet, any web addresses or links contained in this book may have changed since publication and may no longer be valid. The views expressed in this work are solely those of the author and do not necessarily reflect the views of the publisher, and the publisher hereby disclaims any responsibility for them.

The author of this book does not dispense medical advice or prescribe the use of any technique as a form of treatment for physical, emotional, or medical problems without the advice of a physician, either directly or indirectly. The intent of the author is only to offer information of a general nature to help you in your quest for emotional and spiritual well-being. In the event you use any of the information in this book for yourself, which is your constitutional right, the author and the publisher assume no responsibility for your actions.

Any people depicted in stock imagery provided by Thinkstock are models, and such images are being used for illustrative purposes only.

Certain stock imagery © Thinkstock.

ISBN: 978-1-4525-7938-2 (sc)
ISBN: 978-1-4525-7939-9 (e)

Library of Congress Control Number: 2013914273

Printed in the United States of America.

Balboa Press rev. date: 08/15/2013

TABLE OF CONTENTS

Acknowledgments

To Mom and Dad, thank you both for giving me my foundation with God. I truly appreciate how you taught me to set goals and never give up. The *Meditation & Prayer YDS* project is a testimony to that.

To my sons, David and Seth, the *D* and *S* of *YDS*, I love you both with all my heart and am proud of the men you have become. Always remember to do things that are pleasing to God.

My sisters and brother are a source of support. They are always there to help me with whatever I need.

To my friends Karen, Sarah, and Tobie, who are always there for me, thank you. You love me as I am without judgment.

Danny Hiller, you designed the CD Cover and my logo, which appears on the front cover of this book, as well as my stationery and other stationery items. You put countless hours into this project, making my vision come to life. Your talent is boundless.

Carlos Leyva of The Digital Business, your kind words have become my affirmation: "Steve Jobs once famously said: 'Real artists ship.' You are shipping, so that is VERY COOL!"

Martine of iMprints Graphic Plus, thank you for your creative imagination. The cover and other items you have designed for me are fabulous.

La' Quoia Ivery, thank you for taking the headshot photo. You have a creative eye for the camera.

Dr. Paul Weisser (my favorite Einstein look-alike), you taught me the proper etiquette of editing. Since I am in Texas, and you are in California, you also taught me how to video-conference and screen-share. I am eternally grateful for your wisdom. Your belief in me and your statement of my credentials to teach this *Meditation & Prayer YDS* program, gave me the courage to continue to completion.

My friend, Tatyana, your painting in now a part of this project and will live on forever. Thank you for your friendship during your time on earth. I love you!

Yvette Silva
August 2012

Inspiration and Me

It is my hope that you will release all the hurt buried in your heart enough to allow God's ray of love to enter. His small ray of love is strong enough to manifest deeply to allow you to learn to love yourself, to love others, and ultimately to *trust* God. As stated in scripture, He just needs you to open your heart the size of a mustard seed and He will do the rest.

Alone, my greatest accomplishment has been raising my boys, David and Seth. They have given me; the strength to always endure when I am tired, the encouragement to keep moving forward when I fall, the tenacity to never give up when I am weak, and the vulnerability to know that I must keep learning and improving when I am overloaded. As a result, they have made me a better person.

I have met countless people, who I prefer to call Angels, who have taught me that being a Christian does not make me perfect. It just means that I am forgiven, and that I must learn to forgive myself so I can forgive others as God has forgiven me. Learning to forgive myself was a new concept. I learned that forgiving ourselves is just as important as forgiving others. "To the Lord our God belong mercy and loving kindness and forgiveness, for we have rebelled against Him" (Daniel 9:9, Amplified Bible).

I must say the most important thing I have learned is to trust God. This continues to be a learning process. I am learning to go to Him for all my needs, as in Mark 11:24: "For this reason I am telling you, whatever you ask for in prayer, believe that it is granted to you, and you will (get it)."

Remember, it takes twenty-one days to change a habit. Be good to yourself and give yourself thirty.

You are worth it!

A Love Letter to My Sons

Dear David and Seth,

The entire project of *Meditation & Prayer YDS LLC* is the promise I kept to you, my sons. I promised you both that I would start something that included all three of us.

Our initials are in the center of the cross. It is my hope that God will always watch over all three of us, since our foundation belongs to Him.

One of the things I did right for each of you at an early age, as a single parent, was to give you the foundation of Jesus Christ and of God!

May He watch over both of you wherever you go.

I have taught you both, my sons, that it is okay to fall down. But always get back up, brush yourself off, figure out what you can do differently, accept your responsibility, and move on.

The important thing is to learn how you can improve yourself.

David, Seth, and Mom—we are the three musketeers, always and forever.

You both are my heart; and my world.

I love you, my sons!

—Mom

A Personal Note

Hopping from New Age to Judaism to Buddhism and back to Catholicism, I tried to fill a void in my heart. I have been involved with various religious denominations, even within Christianity. I have appreciated learning the best of all of them. The best of each is still a part of me!

I discovered how important it was for me to change my thought patterns during my journey through New Age. I had the honor of meeting Rob Butts, husband to Jane Roberts, authors of the Seth Material. Their writings are kept in the Yale University archives.

It was the Seth Material that helped me realize how essential it was for me to teach myself to gain strength by going beyond my thought patterns on my trials and tribulations. What I thought about all day would ultimately manifest in my life. So I needed to choose if I was going to think of the negative or the positive things.

In addition, I also had the honor of meeting Shirley MacLaine. Her spiritual journey, she turned into the TV series _Out on a Limb_ gave me hope that I could change my life by thinking positively and bringing joy back into my life. More importantly, she taught me that everything happens for a reason; in both bad and good. My New Age experience continued as I began pasting affirmations all over my room, workplace, and car in my early twenties. This is a practice I continue to this day.

Judaism brought me rich traditions, which are hundreds of years old. It brought me back to reading the Old Testament of the Bible. I was blessed to become a docent, during Chanukah, at the Jewish Community Center. Each room was decorated as if we were reliving the biblical times of Christ. I learned the importance of having _faith,_ as I was telling the story of Chanukah, the one-day supply of oil that lasted for seven days.

My journey through Buddhism taught me to have compassion for my enemies, even when I thought that was a crazy concept. When I was at the temple a Buddhist monk once told me, "Pray for that woman who is tormenting you at work." I resisted at first, realizing that bullying doesn't have an age limit. I went back to my Christian roots and began to pray for her by visualizing God's loving light shining from His heart into hers. The level of compassion that the Dalai Lama has for his enemies is amazing. I hope that I am able to teach my sons this valuable lesson. Buddhism taught me deep meditation, compassion and that peace and happiness come from within.

My foundation of Christianity has taught me so much; I carry these lessons deep in my heart. "For everything that was written in the past was written to teach us, so that through the endurance taught in the Scriptures and the encouragement they provide we might have hope." (Rom. 15:4, New International Version)

And now *my* hope. I am entering an extremely difficult phase of my life—even harder than the hell I endured as a child. Learning to become transparent, it is my hope after you hear my story, you will feel you have a safe place to journey without judgment. I am not a victim. I am a survivor!

It is my hope that you will have peace where you can learn to smile in your heart, have laughter on your face, and love in your life. When you feel anxious, or upset and your thoughts are a runaway train, you now have the tools to get back to normalcy, quick and easy: by referencing the activities in this workbook and CD.

It is not always easy. When I hear my editor reading my autobiography back to me, it seems as if I don't know the person he's talking about. Sometimes hearing it makes me sick and the emotions take a paralyzing grip over my body; causing me to withdraw into my cave, where I am safe from the world. But I know that I have to keep going to continue to learn, to release, and to become whole in every area of my being.

When I was living a double life, keeping all my dark secrets to myself, my stability and sanity came from the support of my family. My parents gave me normalcy and spoiled me rotten with things, vacations. Pretty much anything I wanted. They taught me compassion, by taking in every stray teenager and sharing everything we had with them. The funny thing is, these teenagers had stricter rules living with us than where they came from. Everyone had chores to help the home function. All schoolwork had to be completed and if you didn't have any, you had to study something. This was a tradition that I carried to my children.

My goal is to continue to study the differences of others from the perspective of an accepting heart. Studying Rome will not make me Roman and studying Greece will not make me Greek. No one will ever be able to take God out of my heart. At every stage of my life, I always come back to God.

Meditation & Prayer YDS LLC is *my* spiritual journey

Suggestions for the Workbook

Writing down your story in this workbook will allow you to embrace the emotions that are buried inside. This insight will enable you to make changes that will help you to make a difference in your life. These exercises will help you release the garbage you keep inside. Every day you do the workbook and listen to the CD, you will gain strength from the freedom you are experiencing because you will no longer be burdened. You can't do this in one day or a week and honestly say, "It's not working." You are a work in progress; so don't give up on yourself. This program should become part of your everyday schedule. Keep trying to implement this program until it becomes your daily routine like brushing your teeth. This was written to tap into your auditorial, visual and tactical senses to maximize change.

I suggest that you write your story, your own account of events, as a part of a release, so that you can look back and reflect on how you handle things and why you may react to current situations, which will give you an insight into why you think, feel and act the way you do. Write your story before you listen to your CD, *Meditation & Prayer YDS LLC*. Keep a video diary for the next thirty days about how you felt before and after listening to the CD each day.

Refrain from over-analyzing yourself as you go. Do not spell check or correct grammar; just keep writing until all of your thoughts are out. Do it again and again. Only go back and read what you have written and watch your video diary once your thirty-day journey is over. Then start another thirty-days, do it again and again.

You can write poetry or songs if you wish, but be sure to reflect on your passage from internal hell to internal peace. Every time you release the heavy, painful, negative energy trapped inside you, you will become freer and lighter and the real you will begin to emerge with God's love.

May this workbook be your stepping stone to inner happiness.

Biography contains mature subject matter; parental discretion is advised. If necessary, tear out and continue the positive activities in the workbook.

BIOGRAPHY

(Biography contains mature subject matter. Parental discretion is advised. If necessary, tear out and continue the positive activities in the workbook.)

My name is Yvette Silva. I grew up in a Catholic home, but moved in and out of my relationship with God, as many people do. Being taught to meditate at the age of 14, I never realized that meditation and prayer actually go together. My spiritual journey began on April 22, 2006, the day I rededicated my life to God. The day I walked into Lakewood Church after fifteen years of hopping from New Age to Judaism to Buddhism and back to Catholicism, trying to fill a void in my heart. The moment I walked into the church, I found my home. At the end of the service, the pastor asked all the new visitors to stand up, and then he blessed us and asked us to dedicate one year of our lives to attending the church. I decided to give that year to God first, myself second, and the pastor third.

The first six months in the church were the happiest days of my life, and I felt an inner peace never known before. At that point all the pastors began to preach the importance of trusting God, a new concept for me, and one that I passionately resisted, because I felt that He hadn't protected me when I was young, and that evoked all kinds of emotions. Emotions that I thought were behind me.

I have fond memories of my childhood; I remember growing up riding horses and motorcycles, going on vacations and family functions, etc. The crazy thing is that I was living a double life of happiness and terror. There were things that were out of my control in my life—horrific things, and things that I had to keep to myself.

I discovered early that grownups could be mean, even the ones you are supposed to trust. I experienced sexual abuse and bullying at a very young age, which led me to various self-destructive acts later in life. My innocence was taken away from me when I was five years old. One day, I was playing outside in front of my house, when a stranger suddenly appeared, a Caucasian with dirty blonde hair and green eyes.

"Do you want some candy?" he asked.

"Yes!" I replied enthusiastically.

"Okay, come with me."

He took me by the hand and led me toward a station wagon that was parked in the driveway two houses down from mine.

Opening the back door on the driver's side, he said, "Wait for me here. I'll be right back."

I climbed into the back seat, as instructed, and waited for him to return.

Less than a minute later, he walked out of the house very quickly and climbed into the car beside me. As he looked at me, his eyes seemed to turn red, which scared the hell out of me.

I don't remember what happened after that. The next image I have in my mind is me crying, and hurting terribly between my legs. After he slipped my panties back on me, he grabbed both of my arms very tightly and started shaking me.

"You better not tell anyone," he said. "If you do, I'll come back after you. You're a bad girl!"

He kept repeating this over and over again.

Finally, he let me go.

I ran back home but didn't go inside. Our first nanny was cooking in the kitchen, and I couldn't face her, because I did not want to get in trouble for being a "bad girl". Instead, I stayed outside for a while and cried softly and alone.

Eventually, my older sister came out and saw me.

"Why are you crying?" she asked.

I told her what had just happened. She tried to console me, but she was only nine years old herself, so the advice she gave me was that of a child. She didn't fully understand what had just happened or the physical effects that would come or were related.

I told her what happened and that he said I was a "bad girl".

"It's gonna be okay," she said. "You were a bad girl, but it's gonna be okay."

I felt like I just wanted to disappear off the face of the earth and I begged my sister not to tell my parents. "Please don't tell, please don't tell! Please don't tell Mommy and Daddy I was a bad girl!"

She told me again, "It's gonna be okay."

Finally, I went inside and ran to my room. When it was time for dinner, I still kept everything to myself. My mother had just come home from work and was busy with my youngest sister, who was only one at the time, and my Dad was still off at work.

It wasn't until it was time for my bath that my mother saw the blood on my panties, and became alarmed. She called my Dad, who headed home immediately, and then she called a doctor, who told her to take me to the emergency room. He would meet us.

After the doctor examined me, he told my parents that I had a contagious infection, and they would have to put me in isolation. At the time, there was a hepatitis epidemic going around, and that's what the doctor thought I had. So for the next four or five days, I was surrounded by strangers, who kept sticking needles in me and taking blood samples. All this time, my parents were not allowed in the room to comfort me. When the blood tests came back negative for hepatitis, the doctor decided there must be something wrong with my kidneys. When that theory didn't pan out, he decided I could go home. I was so happy because I was terrified being separated from my parents for so long.

Even friendly strangers are still strangers.

After that, my Mom took me for exams every now and then, but I never had the bleeding problem again, so gradually the episode was forgotten.

For the next twenty-three years, I had night terrors, reliving the events in my sleep. I continued to keep the secrets to myself of what had happened that day with the stranger. I never discussed it again with my sister. I began to wonder if I had imagined the whole thing. It wasn't until my late twenties that I finally asked my mother if she thought I had been sexually abused at five, when she and Dad took me to the hospital. As I was telling her what I remembered, too ashamed to look at her even then. When I finally faced her, she looked at me wide-eyed, and then a tear rolled down her cheek.

I asked her, "Am I crazy, Mom? Or did it really happen?"

She looked at me and replied, "It really did happen. You were bleeding vaginally, but the doctors checked for everything else but that. It never occurred to us back then to think of such a terrible thing."

I went to an elementary school that did not have Hispanics, African Americans, or Asians. Everyone was Caucasian. In second grade, there were three boys who began picking on me for my skin being different. They called me "nigger, blackie, darkie, spear-chucker," and various other derogatory names. I didn't know what those things meant or why they called me them. My juvenile thought was that God had put us all in toasters and left me in a little longer, which was why my skin was brown.

In third grade, those three boys became more taunting and became physical. They would push me, pull my long hair, shoot me with spit wads, and so on. They would knock me down on the playground, which was made of crushed oyster shells. I still have a scar on my knee today. This continued into fourth grade, when they became even bolder. There was a hall between the bathrooms and classrooms. I could not go to the bathroom without two of the boys holding my arms while the third one punched me in the stomach. If I told the teacher, the three boys would always say I started it, and nothing was done. I was afraid to go to the bathroom and this lead to bladder problems.

I remember the day I had enough. I was standing in line for lunch, just outside the classroom. The boys were behind me, taunting and pushing me again, but I pretended to ignore them as if they did not exist, as I had always done for the past two and half years. When I realized that I had left my lunch money in the classroom, I went back to get it. As I turned around, one of the boys stuck his foot out and tripped me. I fell on my hands and knees like a dog. Everything seemed to be in slow motion as I looked up and saw everyone laughing and pointing down at me. I felt pain from my knee, and when I lifted it, I could see blood coming from the scab that was already there from having been knocked down by these boys before. For the first time I defended myself. I beat that boy in the face and stomach and didn't stop. The teacher pulled me off him and sent me to the principal's office. Then, I was the one in trouble again, not the boy who had deliberately tripped me. Nothing was said of that, only my response to it.

A few weeks later, one of the boys began bullying me again in the classroom by throwing spit wads and hitting me with a ruler. The teacher seemed to be blind and deaf. She was oblivious and didn't notice him doing this or me asking loudly for him to stop repeatedly. When he didn't, I picked up a chair and threw it at him, then another and then a desk. The teacher noticed. I had three years of pent-up anger from being bullied by those boys, which was never addressed by any of the teachers. My parents had to come to the school to get me. Again, nothing happened to the boy who had started the bullying.

Several months later, a teacher asked me to take a folder to another teacher. The folder had my name on it, so on the way, I opened it and read: "Yvette has a problem with being Mexican." That is what went in my permanent school file, not the truth. I don't remember the teachers' or the boys' names. There was nothing in there about the boys picking on me.

While being bullied at school, I was also enduring sexual abuse at home from the hands of someone I should have been able to trust.

One of our nannies made me take naps with her. She would always tell me I was her favorite, and I was special. I remember her lying down with me on a twin bed. She would tell me that she was going to make me feel good as she proceeded to slip her hand inside my panties. When she was done, she would change her demeanor and tell me I better not tell anyone, or she would say I was a "bad girl." I never did tell anyone. Once again, I was the "bad girl."

It wasn't until 2006 that I asked my mom about it. She was on the phone, so I mouthed the question, "How long was the nanny with us?" My mom said three years. My mind blocked it out. I went home to my own house and cried in the shower, yelling at God for not protecting me.

As years passed, I encountered my former nanny. With children of my own, I would not let them out of my sight or give her a chance to be alone with them. Being near her made me nervous. I still recall when she came up behind me and put her hands on my shoulders. I froze. My mind went blank instantly and I was paralyzed all over. It took all my might to pull away from her touch. I did not want her hands on my children or me. I thought about the incident later and could not believe how I was instantly a child again with just the touch of her hands on my shoulders.

I thought it would be over when the nanny left us. It never seemed to stop! Unexpectedly, God put another obstacle in my path.

During my pre-teen years, there was a family friend who called me over to him while at a gathering. He smelled of alcohol as he pulled me between his legs and put his hands up my shirt. He pulled his hands out quickly, as if he were disappointed. I had not yet begun to develop. He pulled my shorts and panties down and I knew what was coming next. When his hand touched my vagina, I froze and blanked out. When he was done, he pulled up my panties. He grabbed my arms and shook me hard and gave me the warning I had heard repeatedly before, since the age of five, "I better not tell anyone." When I didn't answer, he shook me again, and I could smell the alcohol on his breath. I said, "Okay," and then ran away, again keeping the incident to myself. By the end of grade school, I knew the drill.

My perception of trust was skewed by this time. A sense of normalcy was not in my comprehension.

I was very angry at God, myself, and everyone who hurt me. Keeping everything in was brewing inside my soul like a teakettle ready to whistle when the water boils.

So, when I became older, in the eighth grade, I turned to drugs to mask the pain. Alcohol came later. I just wanted to numb all my secrets, but they always came out in night terrors.

There were more infractions to my soul. It seemed as if they were never going to end. All the while, I kept them to myself. It was as if I had two lives, one of lonely hell and the other of being raised with a silver spoon.

I know there are stories that are worse than mine, but this is my story. This is my fight for happiness, sanity, and peace. It is not easy being transparent; it is physically difficult. However, if it will help one person to fight and not give up on happiness, sanity, and peace, it will be worth it.

CHAPTER 1

WHAT'S YOUR STORY?

Recall Your Defining Moment

WHAT'S YOUR STORY?

Recall your defining moment

Take your time with this. You can write all at once or a little bit at a time. Do this at your own comfort level. Only you are able to write about the pain that lingers in your heart. Be honest with yourself about the events that caused you heartbreak so you can release it once and for all. Use only first names or an initial of the people you are writing about. This is about releasing your pain and not causing turmoil to others or revenge. (For reinforcement see Chapter 5: Release)

The more you release out of your heart by writing, sharing, or helping someone else who has a similar pain, the more you will begin to let go. Soon you will be releasing the internal garbage of your heart, which will in turn clear your mind. This will make room for the positive affirmations to take root. (For enhancement see Chapters 6: I Am and Chapter 7: Living in the Present)

You can share your story with the world, or you don't have to share it with anyone. You can even write a letter to God, I just happen to have His address. Remember to leave out complete names, and mail it to Him at:

> God
> 100 Sugar St.
> Heaven, Universe 77777

Do whatever you are comfortable with as you write your story.

May God be with you as you begin to release and free your heart. (For enrichment see Chapter 8: God's Time.)

Prayer Is Speaking to God. Meditation Is Listening to God.™

MY STORY

Page 1

_____

_____

_____

_____

_____

_____

_____

_____

_____

_____

_____

_____

_____

_____

_____

_____

_____

_____

_____

_____

_____

_____

MY STORY

Page 2

_____

_____

_____

_____

_____

_____

_____

_____

_____

_____

_____

_____

_____

_____

_____

_____

_____

_____

_____

_____

_____

_____

_____

_____

_____

MY STORY

Page 3

_____

_____

_____

_____

_____

_____

_____

_____

_____

_____

_____

_____

_____

_____

_____

_____

_____

_____

_____

_____

_____

_____

_____

_____

_____

_____

MY STORY

Page 4

_____

_____

_____

_____

_____

_____

_____

_____

_____

_____

_____

_____

_____

_____

_____

_____

_____

_____

_____

_____

_____

_____

_____

_____

_____

_____

MY STORY

Page 5

_____

_____

_____

_____

_____

_____

_____

_____

_____

_____

_____

_____

_____

_____

_____

_____

_____

_____

_____

_____

_____

_____

_____

_____

MY STORY

Page 6

_____

_____

_____

_____

_____

_____

_____

_____

_____

_____

_____

_____

_____

_____

_____

_____

_____

_____

_____

_____

_____

_____

_____

_____

MY STORY

Page 7

_____

_____

_____

_____

_____

_____

_____

_____

_____

_____

_____

_____

_____

_____

_____

_____

_____

_____

_____

_____

_____

_____

_____

_____

CHAPTER 2

SELF-BELIEF

Think About What You Believe

WHO DO YOU THINK YOU ARE?

Think About What You Believe

The next few pages are for you to be aware of your own self-perception. In the following statements, there is no right or wrong answer, only what you believe about yourself.

Answer the questions as quickly as you can, and do not give them any thought. Your first answer is usually the most truthful. Do not read or review it.

This is a survey to determine where you are before you begin the Meditation & Prayer YDS program. Answer the questions as rapidly as you can without taking a great deal of time and consideration. The following statements will focus on your own perceptions, thoughts and feelings.

Save your first survey and then take it again after completing the thirty-day exercises *Meditation & Prayer YDS* program.

This is only for you.

Prayer Is Speaking to God. Meditation Is Listening to God.™

WHO DO YOU THINK YOU ARE?

Day One—Date: _____ **Time:** _____

✓ I think I am smart. ....Yes   No

✓ I think I am stupid. ....Yes   No

✓ I think I am ugly. ....Yes   No

✓ I think I am pretty. ....Yes   No

✓ I think I am beautiful. ....Yes   No

✓ I think I am sad. ....Yes   No

✓ I think I am lonely. ....Yes   No

✓ I think I am happy. ....Yes   No

✓ I think I am joyful. ....Yes   No

✓ I think I am poor. ....Yes   No

✓ I think I am rich. ....Yes   No

✓ I think I am selfish. ....Yes   No

✓ I think I am helpful. ....Yes   No

✓ I think I am honest. ....Yes   No

✓ I think I am dishonest. ....Yes   No

✓ I think I am full of energy. ....Yes   No

✓ I think I am low in energy. ....Yes   No

✓ I think I am forgiving. ....Yes   No

✓ I think I hold a grudge. ....Yes   No

✓ I think I don't stay mad. ....Yes   No

✓ I think I stay mad. ....Yes   No

✓ I think I like people. ....Yes   No

✓ I think I don't like people. ....Yes   No

✓ I think I am faithful. ....Yes   No

✓ I think I am realistic. ....Yes   No

✓ I think I am resentful. ....Yes   No

✓ I think I am tolerant. ....Yes   No

✓ I think I am self-centered. ....Yes   No

✓ I think I am wealthy. ....Yes   No

✓ I think I am neat. ....Yes   No

✓ I think I am messy. ....Yes   No

✓ I think I dress nicely. ....Yes   No

✓ I think how I dress is unimportant. ....Yes   No

✓ I think I am lost. ....Yes   No

✓ I think I am bitter. ....Yes   No

✓ I think I am unfocused. ....Yes   No

✓ I think I have made many mistakes. ....Yes   No

✓ I think I lack concentration. ....Yes   No

✓ I think I should be first. ....Yes   No

✓ I think I am confused. ....Yes   No

✓ I think I am sad. ....Yes   No

✓ I think I am tired of living. ....Yes   No

✓ I think I will never be happy. ....Yes   No

✓ I think sometimes I can laugh. ....Yes   No

✓ I think it is hard to get up in the morning. ....Yes   No

✓ I think I can never learn. ....Yes   No

✓ I think I can be better. ....Yes   No

✓ I think I am open to trying new things. ....Yes   No

✓ I think I learn easily. ....Yes   No

✓ I think I like easy steps when I learn. ....Yes   No

✓ I think I want to be happy. ....Yes   No

✓ I think I want to like myself. ....Yes   No

✓ I think I want others to like me. ....Yes   No

✓ I think I want to teach others. ....Yes   No

✓ I think I want to take care of myself. ....Yes   No

✓ I think I am ready to let go of anger. ....Yes   No

✓ I think I am ready to forgive others. ....Yes   No

✓ I think I am ready to forgive myself. ....Yes   No

WHO DO YOU THINK YOU ARE?

Day Thirty—Date: _____ **Time:** _____

✓ I think I am smart. ....Yes   No

✓ I think I am stupid. ....Yes   No

✓ I think I am ugly. ....Yes   No

✓ I think I am pretty. ....Yes   No

✓ I think I am beautiful. ....Yes   No

✓ I think I am sad. ....Yes   No

✓ I think I am lonely. ....Yes   No

✓ I think I am happy. ....Yes   No

✓ I think I am joyful. ....Yes   No

✓ I think I am poor. ....Yes   No

✓ I think I am rich. ....Yes   No

✓ I think I am selfish. ....Yes   No

✓ I think I am helpful. ....Yes   No

✓ I think I am honest. ....Yes   No

✓ I think I am dishonest. ....Yes   No

✓ I think I am full of energy. ....Yes   No

✓ I think I am low in energy. ....Yes   No

✓ I think I am forgiving. ....Yes   No

✓ I think I hold a grudge. ....Yes   No

✓ I think I don't stay mad. ....Yes   No

✓ I think I stay mad. ....Yes   No

✓ I think I like people. ....Yes No

✓ I think I don't like people. ....Yes No

✓ I think I am faithful. ....Yes No

✓ I think I am realistic. ....Yes No

✓ I think I am resentful. ....Yes No

✓ I think I am tolerant. ....Yes No

✓ I think I am self-centered. ....Yes No

✓ I think I am wealthy. ....Yes No

✓ I think I am neat. ....Yes No

✓ I think I am messy. ....Yes No

✓ I think I dress nicely. ....Yes No

✓ I think how I dress is unimportant. ....Yes No

✓ I think I am lost. ....Yes No

✓ I think I am bitter. ....Yes No

✓ I think I am unfocused. ....Yes No

✓ I think I have made many mistakes. ....Yes No

✓ I think I lack concentration. ....Yes No

✓ I think I should be first. ....Yes No

✓ I think I am confused. ....Yes No

✓ I think I am sad. ....Yes No

✓ I think I am tired of living. ....Yes No

✓ I think I will never be happy. ....Yes No

✓ I think sometimes I can laugh. ....Yes No

✓ I think it is hard to get up in the morning. ....Yes No

✓ I think I can never learn. ....Yes   No

✓ I think I can be better. ....Yes   No

✓ I think I am open to trying new things. ....Yes   No

✓ I think I learn easily. ....Yes   No

✓ I think I like easy steps when I learn. ....Yes   No

✓ I think I want to be happy. ....Yes   No

✓ I think I want to like myself. ....Yes   No

✓ I think I want others to like me. ....Yes   No

✓ I think I want to teach others. ....Yes   No

✓ I think I want to take care of myself. ....Yes   No

✓ I think I am ready to let go of anger. ....Yes   No

✓ I think I am ready to forgive others. ....Yes   No

✓ I think I am ready to forgive myself. ....Yes   No

COURSE OPINION QUESTIONNAIRE

When answering the next series of questions, be honest because there are no right or wrong answers, only *your* answers. Answer the questions as quickly as you can without thinking too deeply. Do not read or review your responses until you have completed the thirty days.

As you respond to the questions, see if they evoke any emotions. Where are those emotions coming from? Make a note if the emotion is one that is still lingering from the past and needs to be eliminated.

This questionnaire will get you thinking about your beliefs about God and how you deal with issues in your life.

Prayer Is Speaking to God. Meditation Is Listening to God.™

COURSE OPINION QUESTIONNAIRE

- When I think of praying to God, I think of:

  _____

  _____

- Some of the reasons I pray to God are:

  _____

  _____

- What was the last positive thought I had?

  _____

  _____

- How many ways have I tried to make changes in my life, how?

  _____

  _____

- When I think of the word *prayer*, I feel:

  _____

  _____

- If I could say a prayer right now, I would pray about:

  _____

  _____

- To me, the word *meditate* means:

  _____

  _____

- When I think of the act of meditation, I think of:

_____

_____

- Do I know how to meditate?

_____

_____

- Did I know that the words *meditate* and *meditation* are in the Bible?

_____

_____

- Which Bible verse combines the importance of meditation and the words that I speak?

_____

_____

- What is in my heart will be the words that I speak. Do I know the Bible verse that proves this?

_____

_____

- What does the Bible say about anxiety?

_____

_____

- The definition of anxiety is "painful or apprehensive uneasiness of mind, fearful concern or interest." Have I ever felt anxiety or stress at any time in my life?

_____

_____

- Can I vividly recall a time when I was anxious or stressed? How did that make me feel? How long ago was it, and does it still hurt today?

_____

_____

- What process do I go through to eliminate hurt?

_____

_____

- Do my thoughts replay painful events over and over again?

_____

_____

- "A calm and undisturbed mind and heart are the life and health of the body, but envy, jealousy, and wrath are like rottenness of the bones." (Proverbs 14:20)
  This verse speaks of the mind, heart and body and then of envy, jealousy and wrath. What does this verse mean to me?

_____

_____

- What was the last positive act of kindness I did for someone else?

_____

_____

- What was the last kind word I said to someone else?

_____

_____

- I know I am ready to commit to thirty days of trying something new because:

_____

_____

CHAPTER 3

———⁓◦⊰⊙⊱◦⁓———

MY CHANGES

*Take Accountability of Your Life
to Make Changes*

MY CHANGES

Take Accountability for Your Life to Make Changes

Take a moment to review the things you are doing in your daily life. Change requires using good judgment with moderation.

When you spend to much time watching television, this is not good for developing a positive attitude. Watching shows with negative messages and depressing content can make you depressed. Speaking from my own personal experiences, watching these types of shows kept me from releasing sad, depressing emotions. Clearly, it kept me stuck. Do you find yourself in this situation? Is this you?

Now is the time to stop watching those programs with violence, deception and trauma. Please note that I am not saying to stop watching television or the news; select programs that put you in a good positive mindset that encourages change and hope. Again, use discretion with what you are feeding your mind, especially when you are feeling stressed and depressed.

As you change your behavior and habits remember to put affirmations everywhere. By keeping them in sight, they will severe as reminders for you. Every time you see one, verbalize it out loud. I used this technique and this helped me to get through a lot of turmoil in my own life. I still use this method today.

I'm just like any other person that enjoys listening to all types of music, including rock 'n' roll, but I also know that listening to certain types of music all of the time has the same affect as a negative television program. There is always a time and a place for everything, including music so find a genre that relaxes you, so when you do have those days of stress, you can listen to the music on your way home from work and you can listen to *Meditation & Prayer YDS* when you get home.

If you really want to make changes in your life, you need to take inventory of the words that come out of your mouth. That is easier said than done, but it is part of the process of making positive changes. When you catch yourself saying negative words, immediately replace them with positive ones. You are becoming aware, and that is a good thing for change. Also, notice what the people around you are saying. Remember that misery loves company. Is your company miserable? Always lend a tender ear because everyone needs to get things out, but then it is time for you to hold a mirror up to whoever is keeping you down.

Have you ever seen individuals who are always happy? They don't criticize other people, they don't talk behind their backs, and they always have a song in their heart. Those are the people you want to hang around with. Sometimes that will mean removing yourself from a group, from family, from co-workers, or from whoever else is dragging you down. Remember to pray for their happiness.

The best thing you can do is to find someone who needs mentoring. When you are helping someone else, you are not so focused on your own problems. Find programs in your community that will help or guide teenagers. The elderly can be found in your neighborhood or in a nursing home. They would love a visitor or someone to speak with, perhaps a change of scenery like the mall, a movie, or the grocery store. In Chapter 13, you will find Happy Cards. Keep these with you, pass them out, and put a smile on someone's face.

Take a walk to clear your mind. You can walk in the mall, park, or gym.

Tell those you love that you love them. Tomorrow may be too late.

Look in the mirror and repeat the various affirmations in this workbook to yourself. "I am worth it!" That is the most important exercise you can do for yourself!

You really want to think about this. Think about all of the changes you want to make in your life. Some of these changes will be easy, and others will be difficult. The main thing is that you are trying.

You will be able to achieve some of your changes quickly, but others will take longer. That is okay! Just keep trying until you accomplish your goals and results in your life. You may start your CD now and listen to Track 1 through Track 3.

Prayer Is Speaking to God. Meditation Is Listening to God.™

TRACK 1—GREETING

Hello, I'm Yvette Silva.

Welcome to Meditation & Prayer. I have been a meditation practitioner since 1978. I believe meditation and prayer go together on a daily basis. I am now combining meditation and prayer together on this CD. Prayer is speaking to God, and meditation is listening to God.

I was inspired to write this audio program as a direct result of my own experiences through meditation and prayer with God.

For individually designed private meditation sessions, email silvauniverse@yahoo.com.

Please be sure to put: "Private Sessions" in the subject line.

Be sure to include your name and evening phone number.

Website: www.mpyds.com

Facebook Page: Meditation & Prayer YDS

TRACK 2—INTRODUCTION

I would like to congratulate you on your first step to making positive changes in your own life. There are 365 days in a year, and you are making a thirty-day commitment to yourself. Make the commitment to listen to this Meditation & Prayer CD every night for thirty consecutive days.

Research has shown that it takes only twenty-one days to change a habit. I recommend giving yourself a commitment of thirty days. You are worth it!

In Session One, I will introduce twelve very important preparation points for you to remember. So *write them down*. (Refer to Track 3: Guidelines)

In Session Two, you will be guided through a step-by-step process of how to begin your Meditation & Prayer experience. (Refer to Track 4: Meditation Steps)

Session Three is a guided meditation for clearing old tapes and patterns in your thought process that no longer serve you, so you can create the space for the *good* to manifest in your life. (Refer to Track 5: Release)

In Session Four, you will be redefining the true you and claiming your empowerment. (Refer to Track 6: I Am)

Session Five offers support to move forward with a new direction in your life by learning to live in the present. (Refer to Track 7: Living in the Present)

Session Six is your time with God! Through these encouraging Bible verses, you will gain the reassurance that His love and power are with you on your new journey. (Refer to Track 8: God's Time)

TRACK 3—GUIDELINES

Session One

There are numerous things you can do to help yourself experience positive changes in your life. Here are twelve very important points to remember, so write them down.

1. Turn off the TV set.
2. Stop watching the news or anything else with severe violence.
3. Put affirmations anywhere you can read them, all day long. Put them on your bathroom mirror, by your bed, in your car, on your computer at work and at home, and on your refrigerator. Repeat these affirmations over and over every time you see them.
4. Listen to soothing music.
5. Be aware of the statements that you are making. Are they positive or negative? When you catch yourself saying something negative, reword it to be positive.
6. Surround yourself with positive people.
7. Pray.
8. Become a positive role model in someone else's life.
9. Spend your time in an organization that needs volunteers to help others.
10. Walk or exercise twenty to thirty minutes every day.
11. Tell your family and friends that you love them, every day.
12. While looking into a mirror, repeat the daily affirmations to yourself.

The choice is *yours!*

It is ideal to listen to this CD in the morning and at night, but if you are unable to do both, the evening time would be better. It is especially great to listen to it after work or whenever you need a pick-me-up.

MY CHANGES

Write down the changes you want to make in your life:

Check when completed.

☐ 1. Turn off the TV set._____

☐ 2. Stop watching news or anything else with violence. _____

☐ 3. Read inspiring affirmations all day. _____

☐ 4. Listen to soothing music. _____

☐ 5. Change negative statements into positive ones. _____

☐ 6. Surround yourself with positive people. _____

☐ 7. Pray every day. _____

☐ 8. Be a positive role model or mentor for another person. _____

☐ 9. Volunteer to help others. _____

☐ 10. Walk or exercise twenty to thirty minutes every day. _____

☐ 11. Tell your family and friends that you love them, every day. _____

☐ 12. Look in the mirror and repeat affirmations. _____

☐ 13. Listen to the Meditation & Prayer YDS CD. _____

☐ 14. _____

☐ 15. _____

☐ 16. _____

☐ 17. _____

☐ 18. _____

☐ 19. _____

☐ 20. _____

- [ ] 21. _____
- [ ] 22. _____
- [ ] 23. _____
- [ ] 24. _____
- [ ] 25. _____
- [ ] 26. _____
- [ ] 27. _____
- [ ] 28. _____
- [ ] 29. _____
- [ ] 30. _____
- [ ] 31. _____
- [ ] 32. _____
- [ ] 33. _____
- [ ] 34. _____
- [ ] 35. _____
- [ ] 36. _____
- [ ] 37. _____
- [ ] 38. _____
- [ ] 39. _____
- [ ] 40. _____
- [ ] 41. _____
- [ ] 42. _____
- [ ] 43. _____
- [ ] 44. _____

☐ 45. _____

☐ 46. _____

☐ 47. _____

☐ 48. _____

☐ 49. _____

☐ 50. _____

☐ 51. _____

☐ 52. _____

☐ 53. _____

☐ 54. _____

☐ 55. _____

☐ 56. _____

☐ 57. _____

☐ 58. _____

☐ 59. _____

THIRTY-DAY CALENDAR

Take Accountability for Your Life to Make Changes

It is proven that it takes twenty-one days to change a habit, so give yourself thirty days.

Put the calendar in a place where you will be able to listen to the Meditation & Prayer YDS CD in the morning, during lunch time, or before bedtime. Be sure to take notes or record your thoughts and reactions to the meditation sessions.

When you think about taking time for your self-improvement, think of this on a grander scale. There are 365 days in a year. Give yourself thirty days, fifteen to twenty minutes each day to listen to the CD. Invest time in you and your self-fulfillment.

You are the only person who can make changes in your life by taking time to commit to Meditation & Prayer YDS.

Prayer Is Speaking to God. Meditation Is Listening to God.™

THIRTY DAY CALENDAR

	Sunday	Monday	Tuesday	Wednesday	Thursday	Friday	Saturday

(Insert the month you start in the blank box.)

CHAPTER 4

HOW TO MEDITATE

Step-By-Step on What To Do

TRACK 4—MEDITATION STEPS

Session Two

If you know how to meditate, listen to this CD in a meditative state in order to start changing the old tapes in your head. Do it again for the same amount of time, morning and evening. You want to repeat the words in the exercises either out loud or quietly to yourself. You will then take a deep breath to maintain the meditative state. You will be guided as to when to breathe.

If you are not sure how to meditate, or you are trying to do it for the first time, I will walk you through the basics steps. If you find when you are meditating that you have lost track of time when you are meditating, you are doing it correctly. If you fall asleep, that is okay too. It just means your body needs rest.

1. You may not always find a place to lie down, so it is a good idea to learn how to meditate sitting up.
2. In a sitting position, look straight ahead. Then only move your eyes by looking up at a 45-degree-angle. A good focus would be at the point where the wall and the ceiling meet. Then close your eyelids, still keeping your eyes pointed in the direction of the 45-degree-angle. This puts your brain in a receptive mode for deep relaxation.
3. Place your hands comfortably on your lap. Keep them relaxed.
4. Inhale through your nose and exhale through your mouth—slowly, three times. I will show you how. Concentrate on your breathing to relax physically. Listen.
5. Remember to keep your eyes looking up at a 45-degree-angle while your eyelids remain closed.
6. When you close your eyes, close them lightly. Do not put any strain or pressure on them. In other words, do not squint.
7. Once again, inhale through your nose and exhale through your mouth—slowly, three times. Listen to the air going into your nose and coming out of your mouth to relax mentally.

You can move, adjust, scratch, or cough if you need to. You are not locked into this position. It's okay to open your eyes; just be sure to go back to the position and repeat the deep breathing exercises. Remember to keep your eyes at a 45-degree-angle.

Periodically, inhale through your nose and exhale through your mouth, deeply.

Practice doing steps one through nine on your own a few times to get the feel of relaxing. As you slow down your breathing, you also slow down your heart rate. When you feel like you are able to slow down your breathing and your heart rate, you are ready to listen to the Meditation & Prayer CD. Put yourself in a relaxing, meditative state and begin your exercises.

Remember to say a prayer before or after you meditate, always giving thanks to God. Happiness is a choice, and the choice is *yours*.

CHAPTER 5

RELEASE

Get Rid of Negative Thoughts

RELEASE

Get Rid of Negative Emotions

If we keep negative emotions inside our hearts they can lead to depression, anxiety, overeating, under eating, smoking, drinking, cussing, and arguing with people that we know and love for no reason.

When you feel the negative emotions and are unable to release them after your allotted three days to vent, listen to the Guided Release Affirmations. Follow this up by completing the Release Activity sheet listing the negative emotions that you want to release. Repeat this as many times as you wish, especially when you are still feeling anxious, depressed, or upset with negative emotions that arise from life situations from work or home.

If you harbor hate in your heart, the only person it hurts is *you*. Other people may not even be aware of your hate. It's time to let it go and release it. Pray for strength and pray for the person you are angry with. *This* is pleasing to God.

"Let the words of my mouth and the mediation of my heart be acceptable in Your sight, O Lord, my [firm, impenetrable] Rock and my Redeemer." (Psalm 19:14)

Mind your heart by offering forgiveness to whomever your issue is with. But just as important—or even more important—is to forgive yourself. Remember the good times and focus on those. If your only focus is on negative events, you will keep yourself from growing and becoming happy and healthy. You may start your CD now and listen to Track 5 Release.

TRACK 5—RELEASE

Session Three

Look up at a 45-degree-angle and then close your eyes. Inhale through your nose and exhale through your mouth, slowly.

Repeat these phrases after me, silently or out loud:

I release all stress.

I release all tension.

I release all tightness.

I release all stiffness.

I release all friction.

I release all conflict.

I release all dread.

Relax. Take a deep breath. Inhale through your nose and exhale through your mouth. Let's continue to release:

I release all negativity.

I release all pessimism.

I release all destruction.

I release all depression.

I release all despair.

I release all sadness.

I release all misery.

Relax. Take a deep breath. Inhale through your nose and exhale through your mouth. Let's continue to release:

I release all hopelessness.

I release all guilt.

I release all fault.

I release all blame.

I release all shame.

I release all remorse.

I release all anger.

Relax. Take a deep breath. Inhale through your nose and exhale through your mouth. Let's continue to release:

I release all irritation.

I release all fury.

I release all rage.

I release all pressure.

I release all strain.

I release all burden.

I release all anxiety.

Relax. Take a deep breath. Inhale through your nose and exhale through your mouth. Let's continue to release:

I release all concern.

I release all nervousness.

I release all trauma.

I release all weight.

I release all worry.

I release all hassle.

I release all of the past.

Relax. Take a deep breath. Inhale through your nose and exhale through your mouth. Let's continue to release:

I release all envy.

I release all jealousy.

I release all bad thoughts.

I release all nightmares.

I release all illnesses.

I release all debt.

Relax. Take a deep breath. Inhale through your nose and exhale through your mouth. Let's continue to release:

I release all negative beliefs with money.

I release all resentment.

I release all bitterness.

I release all hatred.

I release all offenses.

You may open your eyes. You just experienced a really good release.

(Reaffirm by beginning your Release Activity sheet)

RELEASE ACTIVITY SHEET

Write down the negative emotions you want to release:

I release all _____

I release all _____

I release all _____

I release all _____

I release all _____

I release all _____

I release all _____

I release all _____

I release all _____

I release all _____

I release all _____

I release all _____

I release all _____

I release all _____

I release all _____

I release all _____

I release all _____

I release all _____

I release all _____

I release all _____

I release all _____

I release all _____

CHAPTER 6

I AM

Affirmations to Be Strong

'I AM'

Affirmations to Be Strong

There was a time in my life when I experienced hopelessness and a sense of loss. To make a big change, I used the affirmations. It became easier and easier as I used them daily. I currently have four in my office today.

Only you can change the *belief* in your heart. Remember that you are worth loving, you are strong, you will make it, you will get through it, and you will persevere. Find the affirmations that resonate with you and repeat them while looking in the mirror. Do not give up. When you convince the person staring back at you, you have achieved a change.

Complete I Am Activity Sheet after you finish the I Am CD. Doodle on everything, "I am smart, I am worth loving," etc.

If you say something negative about yourself, immediately replace it with a positive affirmation, something more pleasing. Remember to keep your thoughts and words positive.

Use the affirmation cutout cards in the back of the workbook to reinforce your changes, (Chapter 13). Put them everywhere. You may start your CD now and listen to Track 6.

Prayer Is Speaking to God. Meditation Is Listening to God.™

TRACK 6—I AM

Session Four

Look up at a 45-degree-angle, then close your eyes. Inhale through your nose and exhale through your mouth, slowly.

Repeat these phrases after me, silently or out loud:

I am blessed.

I am happy.

I am content.

I am pleased.

I am glad.

I am joyful.

I am cheerful.

I am in high spirits.

Relax. Take a deep breath, inhale through your nose, now exhale through your mouth. Let's continue to reaffirm ourselves:

I am blissful.

I am ecstatic.

I am delighted.

I am cheerful.

I am jovial.

I am lucky.

I am fortunate.

Relax. Take a deep breath, inhale through your nose, now exhale through your mouth. Let's continue to reaffirm ourselves:

I am privileged.

I am well off.

I am prosperous.

I am favorable.

I am good.

I am worthy.

I am credible.

Relax. Take a deep breath, inhale through your nose, now exhale through your mouth. Let's continue to reaffirm ourselves:

I am helpful.

I am cooperative.

I am useful.

I am sound.

I am beneficial.

I am clever.

I am bright.

Relax. Take a deep breath, inhale through your nose, now exhale through your mouth. Let's continue to reaffirm ourselves:

I am smart.

I am knowledgeable.

I am sharp.

I am trustworthy.

I am reliable.

I am honest.

I am nice.

Relax. Take a deep breath, inhale through your nose, now exhale through your mouth. Let's continue to reaffirm ourselves:

I am gentle.

I am calm.

I am tender.

I am mellow.

I am peaceful.

I am polite.

I am polished.

Relax. Take a deep breath, inhale through your nose, now exhale through your mouth. Let's continue to reaffirm ourselves:

I am gracious.

I am able.

I am kind.

I am friendly.

I am patient.

I am happy.

I am stress-free.

Relax. Take a deep breath, inhale through your nose, now exhale through your mouth. Let's continue to reaffirm ourselves:

I am healthy.

I am thoughtful.

I am wealthy.

I am rich.

I am well off.

I am affluent.

I am prosperous.

I am loaded.

I am balanced.

I am responsible.

I am forgiving.

I am blessed.

You may open your eyes and enjoy the positive energy you have just declared.

(Reaffirm by beginning your I Am Activity sheet)

I Am Activity Sheet

Write down the positive emotions you want to express:

I am _____

I am _____

I am _____

I am _____

I am _____

I am _____

I am _____

I am _____

I am _____

I am _____

I am _____

I am _____

I am _____

I am _____

I am _____

I am _____

I am _____

I am _____

I am _____

I am _____

I am _____

CHAPTER 7

LIVING IN THE PRESENT

Let it Go!

LIVING IN THE PRESENT

Let It Go!

I spent a significant amount of time hating my ex-husband. The lesson I learned was not to hold on to negative emotions. By learning to let go of this resentment, I appreciate him for giving me my greatest joy in life: my two sons.

You can not change the past. It is important to let go, move on and live in the here and now. Life should be joyful and meaningful to you and those around you.

Are you talking negatively about things that happened years, or months, or even weeks ago with co-workers, parents, teachers, boyfriends, girlfriends, husbands, wives, or children? I sure did and sometimes still have those negative conversations. You can't change the past. You may have to work really hard on this one, but keep trying. Fake it till you make it. Put on your rose-colored glasses and pray like hell for your bullies.

Focus on something positive or do something kind for someone else, *right now!*

This is the moment that matters.

When you finish listening to Track 7, Living in the Present, complete the exercise. Use the Affirmation Cards (Chapter 13) and put them everywhere. Hang them where you can see them. Let them be the last thing you see at night and the first thing you see in the morning. You may start your CD now and listen to Track 7.

Prayer Is Speaking to God. Meditation Is Listening to God.™

TRACK 7—LIVING IN THE PRESENT

Session Five

Look up at a 45-degree-angle, then close your eyes. Inhale through your nose and exhale through your mouth, slowly.

Repeat these phrases after me, silently or out loud:

I live in the present.

I live in the current.

I live in the flow.

I live in the stream.

I live in the here.

I live at this time.

I live at this point.

Relax. Take a deep breath through your nose, and then exhale through your mouth. Let's continue to live in the present:

I live in the present.

I live in joy.

I live in delight.

I live in happiness.

I live in pleasure.

I live in bliss.

I live in ecstasy.

Relax. Take a deep breath through your nose, and then exhale through your mouth. Let's continue to live in the present:

I live in elation.

I live in the thrill.

I live in the wonder.

I live in the charm.

I live with life.

I live with good timing.

I live with great days.

Relax. Take a deep breath through your nose, and then exhale through your mouth. Let's continue to live in the present:

I live in being.

I live in present existence.

I live with energy.

I live in animation.

I live to play.

I live with hope.

I live with trust.

Relax. Take a deep breath through your nose, and then exhale through your mouth. Let's continue to live in the present:

I live in faith.

I live in optimism.

I live in desire.

I live in expectation.

I live like a child.

I live to dream.

I live with vision.

Relax. Take a deep breath through your nose, and then exhale through your mouth. Let's continue to live in the present:

I live in patience.

I live with imagination.

I live in marvel.

I live to give.

I live to offer.

I live in ambition.

I live in responsibility.

Relax. Take a deep breath through your nose, and then exhale through your mouth. Let's continue to live in the present:

I live in balance.

I live in wealth.

I live in abundance.

I live in prosperity.

I live in fortune.

I live in riches.

I live in means.

I live with treasure.

I live with forgiveness.

You may open your eyes. Repeat this last phrase out loud: "I continue to live and be in the present!"

(Reaffirm by beginning your Living in the Present Activity sheet)

LIVING IN THE PRESENT ACTIVITY SHEET

Write down the "I Live" changes you want to make in your life:

I live _____

I live _____

I live _____

I live _____

I live _____

I live _____

I live _____

I live _____

I live _____

I live _____

I live _____

I live _____

I live _____

I live _____

I live _____

I live _____

I live _____

I live _____

I live _____

I live _____

I live _____

I live _____

CHAPTER 8

SCRIPTURES

To Reiterate—To Reaffirm

Meditation, Words Spoken, and the Heart in the Bible

To Reiterate—To Reaffirm

No matter your age, gender, race or religious affiliation, everyone will go through trials and tribulations. The end result might lead to frustration, disagreement and disappointment.

Give yourself no more than three days to be upset, and then let it go! Listen to tracks five through eight of Meditation & Prayer YDS. You can skip around and start and stop on the CD, pray, walk do whatever you need to do to quickly release the negative emotions.

> The heart of the wise teaches his mouth,
> and adds learning to his lips.
> —Proverbs 16:23

The next few pages are intended to show you that meditation is all throughout the Bible. It is important to be still and to listen. You will see through the scriptures that the words you choose to speak are important in order to please God and yourself. What you choose to keep in your heart is extremely important and may affect your health and beyond.

> Be still and know that I am God.
> —Psalm 46:10

Whatever you are going through, you can find the right scripture that will help you through it. Put several scriptures everywhere. Go to Chapter 13 and select your affirmations, write your favorites, and cut them out. At that point, past them everywhere so you can see them everyday. Remember to repeat them out loud!

The next few pages will show you how meditation is used in the Bible. Scriptures are grouped into Belief and Believe, Meditate and Meditation and Hearts and Words Spoken. Included are pages with scriptures showing you about what to keep in your heart. Remember, if you keep negative emotion in your heart, it will affect your body in negative ways such as insomnia, stress, overeating, under eating, screaming, drinking, smoking, etc.

> Hope deferred makes the heart sick,
> but when the desire is fulfilled, it is a tree of life.
> —Proverbs 13:12

> For as he thinks in his heart, so is he.
> —Proverbs 23:7

There are seven pages of Scripture Affirmation Cards (Chapter 13) in the back of the book for you to use and place everywhere. Place them where you sleep, brush your teeth, on the refrigerator or on the rear view mirror in your car, on your computer at home and at work. You can change them out.

Prayer Is Speaking to God. Meditation Is Listening to God.™

BELIEF AND BELIEVE

✓ **Belief (noun)**: (1) a state or habit of mind in which trust or confidence is placed in some person or thing; (2) something believed; (3) conviction of the truth of some statement or the reality of some being or phenomenon, especially when based on examination of evidence.

✓ **Believe (verb)**: (1a) to have a firm religious faith; (1b) to accept as true, genuine, or real; (2a) to have a firm conviction about the goodness, efficacy, or ability of something; (2b) to accept the word or evidence of.

✓ "For this reason I am telling you, whatever you ask for in prayer, believe (trust and be confident) that it is granted to you, and you will (get it)" (Mark 11:24).

✓ "You are my hiding place and my shield. I hope in Your word" (Psalm 119:114).

✓ "I anticipated the dawning of the morning and cried (in childlike prayer); I hoped in Your word" (Psalm 119:147).

✓ "This I recall to my mind, therefore have I hope" (Lamentations 3:21).

✓ "I know, my God, that you examine our hearts and rejoice when you find integrity there" (1 Chronicles 29:17).

✓ "Because if you acknowledge and confess with your lips that Jesus is Lord and in your heart believe (adhere to, trust in, and rely on the truth) that God raised Him from the dead, you will be saved" (1 Chronicles 29:17).

✓ "For whoever has (spiritual knowledge), to him will be given, and he will be furnished richly so that he will have abundance; but from him who has not, even what he has will be taken away" (Matthew 13:12).

✓ "Beloved, I pray that you may prosper in every way and (that your body) may keep well, even as (I know) your soul keeps well and prospers" (3 John 1:2).

MEDITATE AND MEDITATION

✓ **Meditate (intransitive verb):** (1) to engage in contemplation or reflection; (2) to engage in mental exercise (as concentration on one's breathing or repetition of a mantra) for the purpose of reaching a heightened level of spiritual awareness; **(transitive verb):** (1) to focus one's thoughts on; reflect on or ponder over; (2) to plan or project in the mind.

✓ **Meditation (noun):** the act or process of **meditating**.

✓ "And Isaac went out to meditate and bow down [in prayer] in the open country in the evening; and he looked up and saw that, behold, the camels were coming" (Genesis 24:63).

✓ "Sing to Him, sing praises to Him; meditate on and talk of all His wondrous works and devoutly praise them!" (1 Chronicles 16:9).

✓ "Practice and cultivate and meditate upon these duties; throw yourself wholly into them [as your ministry], so that your progress may be evident to everybody" (1 Timothy 4:15).

✓ "Indeed, you are doing away with [reverential] fear, and you are hindering and diminishing meditation and devotion before God" (Job 15:4).

✓ "This Book of the Law shall not depart out of your mouth, but you shall meditate on it day and night, that you may observe and do according to all that is written in it. For then you shall make your way prosperous, and then you shall deal wisely and have good success" (Joshua 1:8).

✓ "Resolve and settle it in your minds not to meditate and prepare beforehand how you are to make your defense and how you will answer" (Luke 21:14).

✓ "Now when they take you [to court] and put you under arrest, do not be anxious beforehand about what you are to say nor [even] meditate about it; but say whatever is given you in that hour and at the Moment, for it is not you who will be speaking, but the Holy Spirit" (Mark 13:11).

✓ "But his delight and desire are in the law of the Lord, and on His law (the precepts, the instructions, the teachings of God) he habitually meditates (ponders and studies) by day and by night" (Psalm 1:2).

✓ "Why do the nations assemble with commotion [uproar and confusion of voices], and why do the people imagine (meditate upon and devise) an empty scheme?" (Psalm 2:1).

- ✓ "Let the words of my mouth and the meditation of my heart be acceptable in Your sight, O Lord, my [firm, impenetrable] Rock and my Redeemer" (Psalm 19:14).

- ✓ "My mouth shall speak wisdom; and the meditation of my heart shall be understanding" (Psalm 49:3).

- ✓ "I call to remembrance my song in the night; with my heart I meditate and my spirit searches diligently" (Psalm 77:6).

- ✓ "I will meditate also upon all Your works and consider all Your [mighty] deeds" (Psalm 77:12).

- ✓ "May my meditation be sweet to Him; as for me, I will rejoice in the Lord" (Psalm 104:34).

- ✓ "Sing to Him, sing praises to Him; meditate on and talk of all His marvelous deeds and devoutly praise them" (Psalm 105:2).

- ✓ "I will meditate on Your precepts and have respect to Your ways [the paths of life marked out by Your law]" (Psalm 119:15).

- ✓ "Princes also sat and talked against me, but Your servant meditated on Your statutes" (Psalm 119:23).

- ✓ "Make me understand the way of Your precepts; so shall I meditate on and talk of Your wondrous works" (Psalm 119:27).

- ✓ "My hands also will I lift up [in fervent supplication] to Your commandments, which I love, and I will meditate on Your statutes" (Psalm 119:48).

- ✓ "Let the proud be put to shame, for they dealt perversely with me without a cause; but I will meditate on Your precepts" (Psalm 119:78).

- ✓ "Oh, how love I Your law! It is my meditation all the day" (Psalm 119:97).

- ✓ "I have better understanding and deeper insight than all my teachers, because Your testimonies are my meditation" (Psalm 119:99).

- ✓ "My eyes anticipate the night watches and I am awake before the cry of the watchman, that I may meditate on Your word" (Psalm 119:148).

- ✓ "I remember the days of old; I meditate on all Your doings; I ponder the work of Your hands" (Psalm 143:5).

- ✓ "On the glorious splendor of Your majesty and on Your wondrous works I will meditate" (Psalm 145:5).

HEART AND WORDS SPOKEN

✓ "Therefore my heart rejoiced and my tongue exulted exceedingly; moreover, my flesh also will dwell in hope [will enc, pitch its tent, and dwell in hope in anticipation of the resurrection]" (Acts 2:26).

✓ "And Philip said, If you believe with all your heart [if you have a conviction, full of joyful trust, that Jesus is the Messiah and accept Him as the Author of your salvation in the kingdom of God, giving Him your obedience, then] you may. And he replied, I do believe that Jesus Christ is the Son of God" (Acts 8:37).

✓ "Glory in His holy name; let the hearts of those rejoice who seek the Lord!" (1 Chronicles 16:10).

✓ "Now set your mind and heart to seek (inquire of and require as your vital necessity) the Lord your God" (1 Chronicles 22:19).

✓ "Our mouth is open to you, Corinthians [we are hiding nothing, keeping nothing back], and our heart is expanded wide [for you]!" (2 Corinthians 6:11).

✓ "By way of return then, do this for me—I speak as to children—open wide your hearts also [to us]" (2 Corinthians 6:13).

✓ "And these words which I am commanding you this day shall be [first] in your [own] minds and hearts" (Deuteronomy 6:6).

✓ "Therefore you shall lay up these My words in your [minds and] hearts and in your [entire] being, and bind them for a sign upon your hands and as forehead bands between your eyes" (Deuteronomy 11:18).

✓ "But the word is very near you, in your mouth and in your mind and in your heart, so that you can do it" (Deuteronomy 30:14).

✓ "And I applied myself by heart and mind to seek and search out by [human] wisdom all human activity under heaven. It is a miserable business which God has given to the sons of man with which to busy themselves" (Ecclesiastes 1:13).

✓ "Be not rash with your mouth, and let not your heart be hasty to utter a word before God. For God is in heaven, and you are on earth; therefore let your words be few" (Ecclesiastes 5:2).

✓ "May Christ through your faith [actually] dwell (settle down, abide, make His permanent home) in your hearts! May you be rooted deep in love and founded securely on love" (Ephesians 3:17).

✓ "And become useful and helpful and kind to one another, tenderhearted (compassionate, understanding, loving-hearted), forgiving one another [readily and freely], as God in Christ forgave you" (Ephesians 4:32).

✓ "For the fruit (the effect, the product) of the Light or the Spirit [consists] in every form of kindly goodness, uprightness of heart, and trueness of life" (Ephesians 5:9).

✓ "Speak out to one another in psalms and hymns and spiritual songs, offering praise with voices [and instruments] and making melody with all your heart to the Lord" (Ephesians 5:19).

✓ "I have sent him to you for this very purpose, that you may know how we are and that he may console and cheer and encourage and strengthen your hearts" (Ephesians 6:22).

✓ "This is the agreement (testament, covenant) that I will set up and conclude with them after those days, says the Lord: I will imprint My laws upon their hearts, and I will inscribe them on their minds (on their inmost thoughts and understanding)" (Hebrews 10:16).

✓ "Make the heart of this people fat; and make their ears heavy and shut their eyes, lest they see with their eyes and hear with their ears and understand with their hearts and turn again and be healed" (Isaiah 6:10).

✓ "If anyone thinks himself to be religious (piously observant of the external duties of his faith) and does not bridle his tongue but deludes his own heart, this person's religious service is worthless (futile, barren). But if you have bitter jealousy (envy) and contention (rivalry, selfish ambition) in your hearts, do not pride yourselves on it and thus be in defiance of and false to the Truth" (James 1:26).

✓ "So you also must be patient. Establish your hearts [strengthen and confirm them in the final certainty], for the coming of the Lord is very near" (James 5:8).

✓ "Is anyone among you afflicted (ill-treated, suffering evil)? He should pray. Is anyone glad at heart? He should sing praise [to God]" (James 5:13).

✓ "Receive, I pray you, the law and instruction from His mouth and lay up His words in your heart" (Job 22:22).

✓ "My words shall express the uprightness of my heart, and my lips shall speak what they know with utter sincerity" (Job 33:3).

✔ "Peace I leave with you; My [own] peace I now give and bequeath to you. Not as the world gives do I give to you. Do not let your hearts be troubled, neither let them be afraid. [Stop allowing yourselves to be agitated and disturbed; and do not permit yourselves to be fearful and intimidated and cowardly and unsettled.]" (John 14:27).

✔ "If you live in Me [abide vitally united to Me] and My words remain in you and continue to live in your hearts, ask whatever you will, and it shall be done for you" (John 15:7)

✔ "But if anyone has this world's goods (resources for sustaining life) and sees his brother and fellow believer in need, yet closes his heart of compassion against him, how can the love of God live and remain in him?" (1 John 3:17).

✔ "And, beloved, if our consciences (our hearts) do not accuse us [if they do not make us feel guilty and condemn us], we have confidence (complete assurance and boldness) before God" (1 John 3:21).

✔ "So both men sat down and ate and drank together, and the girl's father said to the man, Consent to stay all night and let your heart be merry" (Judges 19:6).

✔ "Let your hearts therefore be blameless and wholly true to the Lord our God, to walk in His statutes and to keep His commandments, as today" (1 Kings 8:61).

✔ "And He glanced around at them with vexation and anger, grieved at the hardening of their hearts, and said to the man, Hold out your hand. He held it out, and his hand was [completely] restored" (Mark 3:5).

✔ "For where your treasure is, there will your heart be also" (Matthew 6:21).

✔ "But whatever comes out of the mouth comes from the heart, and this is what makes a man unclean and defiles [him]" (Matthew 15:18).

✔ "And He replied to him, You shall love the Lord your God with all your heart and with all your soul and with all your mind (intellect)" (Matthew 22:37).

✔ "Since by your obedience to the Truth through the [Holy] Spirit you have purified your hearts for the sincere affection of the brethren, [see that you] love one another fervently from a pure heart" (1 Peter 1:22).

✔ "For I have derived great joy and comfort and encouragement from your love, because the hearts of the saints [who are your fellow Christians] have been cheered and refreshed through you, [my] brother" (Philemon 1:7).

✔ "I am sending him back to you in his own person, [and it is like sending] my very heart" (Philemon 1:12).

✓ "Yes, brother, let me have some profit from you in the Lord. Cheer and refresh my heart in Christ" (Philemon 1:20).

✓ "Making your ear attentive to skillful and godly Wisdom and inclining and directing your heart and mind to understanding [applying all your powers to the quest for it]" (Proverbs 2:2).

✓ "Lean on, trust in, and be confident in the Lord with all your heart and mind and do not rely on your own insight or understanding" (Proverbs 3:5).

✓ "He taught me and said to me, Let your heart hold fast my words; keep my commandments and live" (Proverbs 4:4).

✓ "Let them not depart from your sight; keep them in the center of your heart" (Proverbs 4:21).

✓ "Keep and guard your heart with all vigilance and above all that you guard, for out of it flow the springs of life" (Proverbs 4:23).

✓ "Bind them continually upon your heart and tie them about your neck" (Proverbs 6:21).

✓ "Bind them on your fingers; write them on the tablet of your heart" (Proverbs 7:3).

✓ "The wise in heart will accept and obey commandments, but the foolish of lips will fall headlong" (Proverbs 10:8).

✓ "Wise men store up knowledge [in mind and heart], but the mouth of the foolish is a present destruction" (Proverbs 10:14).

✓ "The lips of the [uncompromisingly] righteous feed and guide many, but fools die for want of understanding and heart" (Proverbs 10:21).

✓ "Anxiety in a man's heart weighs it down, but an encouraging word makes it glad" (Proverbs 12:25).

✓ "Hope deferred makes the heart sick, but when the desire is fulfilled, it is a tree of life" (Proverbs 13:12).

✓ "The heart knows its own bitterness, and no stranger shares its joy" (Proverbs 14:10).

✓ "A calm and undisturbed mind and heart are the life and health of the body, but envy, jealousy, and wrath are like rottenness of the bones" (Proverbs 14:30).

✓ "Wisdom rests [silently] in the mind and heart of him who has understanding, but that which is in the inward part of [self-confident] fools is made known" (Proverbs 14:33).

- ✓ "The lips of the wise disperse knowledge [sifting it as chaff from the grain]; not so the minds and hearts of the self-confident and foolish" (Proverbs 15:7).

- ✓ "A glad heart makes a cheerful countenance, but by sorrow of heart the spirit is broken" (Proverbs 15:13).

- ✓ "Folly is pleasure to him who is without heart and sense, but a man of understanding walks uprightly [making straight his course]" (Proverbs 15:21).

- ✓ "The light in the eyes [of him whose heart is joyful] rejoices the hearts of others, and good news nourishes the bones" (Proverbs 15:30).

- ✓ "Everyone proud and arrogant in heart is disgusting, hateful, and exceedingly offensive to the Lord; be assured [I pledge it] they will not go unpunished" (Proverbs 16:5).

- ✓ "Pleasant words are as a honeycomb, sweet to the mind and healing to the body" (Proverbs 16:24).

- ✓ "A happy heart is good medicine and a cheerful mind works healing, but a broken spirit dries up the bones" (Proverbs 17:22).

- ✓ "For as he thinks in his heart, so is he. As one who reckons, he says to you, eat and drink, yet his heart is not with you [but is grudging the cost]" (Proverbs 23:7).

- ✓ "Yes, my heart will rejoice when your lips speak right things" (Proverbs 23:16).

- ✓ "He who sings songs to a heavy heart is like him who lays off a garment in cold weather and like vinegar upon soda" (Proverbs 25:20).

- ✓ "As in water face answers to and reflects face, so the heart of man to man" (Proverbs 27:19).

- ✓ "He who leans on, trusts in, and is confident of his own mind and heart is a [self-confident] fool, but he who walks in skillful and godly Wisdom shall be delivered" (Proverbs 28:26).

- ✓ "He thinks in his heart, I shall not be moved; for throughout all generations I shall not come to want or be in adversity" (Psalm 10:6).

- ✓ "Let the words of my mouth and the meditation of my heart be acceptable in Your sight, O Lord, my [firm, impenetrable] Rock and my Redeemer" (Psalm 19:14).

- ✓ "May He grant you according to your heart's desire and fulfill all your plans" (Psalm 20:4).

- ✓ "Examine me, O Lord, and prove me; test my heart and my mind" (Psalm 26:2).

- ✓ "Delight yourself also in the Lord, and He will give you the desires and secret petitions of your heart" (Psalm 37:4).

- ✓ "My heart was hot within me. While I was musing, the fire burned; then I spoke with my tongue" (Psalm 39:3).

- ✓ "I delight to do Your will, O my God; yes, Your law is within my heart" (Psalm 40:8).

- ✓ "My mouth shall speak wisdom; and the meditation of my heart shall be understanding" (Psalm 49:3).

- ✓ "Behold, You desire truth in the inner being; make me therefore to know wisdom in my inmost heart" (Psalm 51:6).

- ✓ "The words of his mouth were smoother than cream or butter, but war was in his heart; his words were softer than oil, yet they were drawn swords" (Psalm 55:21).

- ✓ "My heart is fixed, O God, my heart is steadfast and confident! I will sing and make melody" (Psalm 57:7).

- ✓ "I call to remembrance my song in the night; with my heart I meditate and my spirit searches diligently" (Psalm 77:6).

- ✓ "Search me [thoroughly], O God, and know my heart! Try me and know my thoughts!" (Psalm 139:23).

- ✓ "But what does it say? The Word (God's message in Christ) is near you, on your lips and in your heart; that is, the Word (the message, the basis and object) of faith which we preach" (Romans 10:8).

- ✓ "Because if you acknowledge and confess with your lips that Jesus is Lord and in your heart believe (adhere to, trust in, and rely on the truth) that God raised Him from the dead, you will be saved" (Romans 10:9).

- ✓ "And I will raise up for Myself a faithful priest (Priest), who shall do according to what is in My heart and mind. And I will build him a sure house, and he shall walk before My anointed (Anointed) forever" (1 Samuel 2:35).

- ✓ "And Nathan said to the king, Go, do all that is in your heart, for the Lord is with you" (2 Samuel 7:3).

- ✓ "But just as we have been approved by God to be entrusted with the glad tidings (the Gospel), so we speak not to please men but to please God, Who tests our hearts [expecting them to be approved]" (1 Thessalonians 2:4).

✓ "Be happy [in your faith] and rejoice and be glad-hearted continually (always)" (1 Thessalonians 5:16).

✓ "Comfort and encourage your hearts and strengthen them [make them steadfast and keep them unswerving] in every good work and word" (2 Thessalonians 2:17).

✓ "And as for you, brethren, do not become weary or lose heart in doing right [but continue in well-doing without weakening]" (2 Thessalonians 3:13).

✓ "The object and purpose of our instruction and charge is love, which springs from a pure heart and a good (clear) conscience and sincere (unfeigned) faith" (1 Timothy 1:5).

Choose the scriptures that best fit you and place them on the Scripture Affirmation Cards located in Chapter 13 of the book. Place the cards everywhere you can see them: the bathroom, kitchen, car, and work area.

CHAPTER 9

GOD'S TIME

Giving Him Time to Work

GOD'S TIME

Giving Him Time to Work

Locate the Scripture Cards pages found in Chapter 13. The Scripture Cards are larger than the Affirmation Cards which gives you enough space to write as much of any scripture you choose. Select them from Chapter 8 and 9 or choose your own.

Listening to the scriptures on the Meditation & Prayer YDS CD is a great way to know that you are not alone. Lean on Him in your time of need. In addition, lift Him in praise and meditate on His word when things are good. You can meditate on His word on Track 8, in less than nineteen minutes.

I found the most inner peace when I was attending church. However, I am not "Christianese" and would never impose my beliefs on anyone. Also, I respect others' beliefs and differences, especially since I did so much searching around from religion to religion. I have taken away the best of all the religions and philosophies that I have studied and continue to study and realize that we have more similarities, than differences.

Know that God is not responsible for the horrific things that happen in the world. We do that all by ourselves, directly or indirectly.

When you have completed listening to Track 8, God's Time, finish the exercises that follow. The scriptures listed below are categorized for your current need, such as: Comfort, Confidence, Beliefs, Abundance, Faithfulness, Favors, Forgiveness, Fear, Health, Hope, Integrity, and Peace. You can also choose from the list of scriptures from Chapter 8 of the workbook regarding beliefs, meditation, heart, and words spoken.

After you complete this exercise, write a letter to God, thanking Him for all the things you are grateful for in your life. Are you ready to make a concerted effort to make changes in your life? Be thankful that you have the courage that it takes to get through your trials and tribulations. Are you ready to share your story? Be thankful that you have the strength to endure. You may now start your CD and listen to Track 8.

Prayer Is Speaking to God. Meditation Is Listening to God.™

TRACK 8—GOD'S TIME

Session Six

Look up at a 45-degree-angle, then close your eyes. Inhale through your nose and then exhale through your mouth, slowly.

Repeat these phrases after me silently or out loud:

Comfort

Psalm 118:24: "This is the day the Lord has made, and I will rejoice in it."

Genesis 50:21: "Do not be afraid, I will provide for you."

Ruth 2:13: "Let me find favor in your sight, my Lord. For you have comforted me."

Psalm 69:16: "Your loving kindness is sweet and comforting."

Psalm 23:4: "I will fear no evil, for you are with me, your rod and your staff, they comfort me."

Psalm 71:21: "Increase my greatness and turn and comfort me."

Psalm 86:17: "You, Lord, help and comfort me."

Psalm 119:50: "This is my comfort in my affliction, that your promises give me life."

Relax, take a deep breath through your nose, and then exhale through your mouth. Let's continue to live in God's love:

Psalm 118:24: "This is the day the Lord has made, and I will rejoice in it."

Confidence

2 Corinthians 7:6: "I am happy because I now am of good courage."

Galatians 5:10: "I have confidence in the Lord."

Psalm 71:5: "You are my trust from my youth and the source of my confidence."

Psalm 56:3: "I will have confidence in and put my trust and reliance in you."

Beliefs

Mark 11:24: "Whatever you ask for in prayer, believe that it is granted."

2 Chronicles 20:20: "Believe in the Lord your God, and you shall be established."

Psalm 119:66: "Teach me good judgment . . . , for I believe in Your commandments."

Jeremiah 17:7: "Blessed is the man who believes in, trusts in, and relies on the Lord."

Relax, take a deep breath through your nose, and then exhale through your mouth. Let's continue to live in God's love:

Psalm 118:24: "This is the day the Lord has made, and I will rejoice in it."

John 3:15: "Everyone who believes in Him may not perish, but have eternal life and live forever."

Acts 10:43: "Everyone who believes in Him receives forgiveness of sins through His name."

Acts 15:11: "We believe that we are saved through the Grace of the Lord, Jesus."

Romans 10:9: "Confess with your lips that Jesus is Lord and in your heart believe."

1 Corinthians 13:7: "Love bears up under anything and everything that comes, is ever ready to believe the best of every person."

Abundance

2 Chronicles 2:9: "Prepare for me timber in abundance, for the house I am about to build shall be great and wonderful."

Psalm 37:11: "The meek shall inherit the earth and shall delight themselves in abundance of peace."

Psalm 150:2: "Praise Him according to the abundance of His greatness."

Relax, take a deep breath through your nose, and then exhale through your mouth. Continue to live in God's love:

Psalm 118:24: "This is the day the Lord has made, and I will rejoice in it."

Matthew 13:12: "Whoever has spiritual knowledge . . . will have abundance."

Favors

Genesis 18:3:" "I have found favor in your sight."

Genesis 26:24: "I am with you and will favor you with blessings."

Faithfulness

Psalm 119:30: "I have chosen the way of truth and faithfulness."

1 Timothy 1:12: "I give thanks to Him who has granted me strength and made me able, Jesus Christ our Lord."

Forgiveness

Psalm 130:4: "There is forgiveness with You."

Acts 10:43: "Everyone who believes in Him receives forgiveness."

Relax, take a deep breath through your nose, and then exhale through your mouth. Let's continue to live in God's love:

Psalm 118:24: "This is the day the Lord has made, and I will rejoice in it."

Fear

Job 5:21: "You will be safe from slander and have no fear when destruction comes."

Health

Proverbs 16:24: "Pleasant words are as a honeycomb, sweet to the mind and healing to the body."

Isaiah 38:16: "Give me back my health and make me live!"

3 John 1:2: "I pray that you may prosper in every way."

Mark 5:28: "I shall be restored to health."

Hope

Ezra 10:2: "Now there is still hope."

Psalm 71:5: "You are my hope; O Lord God, You are my trust."

Psalm 119:114: "You are my hiding place and my shield, I hope in your word."

Relax, take a deep breath through your nose, and then exhale through your mouth. Let's continue to live in God's love:

Psalm 118:24: "This is the day the Lord has made, and I will rejoice in it."

Psalm 119:147: "I rise before dawn and cry for help, I hope in your words."

Psalm 22:9: "You made me hope and trust."

Lamentations 3:21: "I recall to my mind, and therefore I have hope."

Integrity

Genesis 20:6: "I know you did this in the integrity of your heart."

1 Chronicles 29:17: "I know, my God, that you examine our hearts and rejoice when you find integrity there."

Psalm 25:21: "Let integrity and uprightness preserve me, for I wait for and expect you."

Psalm 26:11: "I will walk in my integrity; redeem me and be merciful and gracious to me."

Relax, take a deep breath through your nose, and then exhale through your mouth. Let's continue to live in God's love:

Psalm 118:24: "This is the day the Lord has made, and I will rejoice in it."

Psalm 101:2: "I will walk within my house in integrity and with a blameless heart."

Psalm 41:12: "You have upheld me in my integrity and set me in Your presence forever."

Job 31:6: "God may know my integrity!"

Psalm 26:1: "O Lord . . . , I have walked in my integrity."

Peace

Galatians 5:22: "The fruit of the Spirit is love, joy, peace, patience, and faithfulness."

Job 22:21: "Acquaint now yourself with Him and be at peace."

Psalm 34:14: "Turn away from evil and do good, seek peace and pursue it."

Psalm 85:10: "Steadfast love and faithfulness meet, righteousness and peace kiss each other."

Relax, take a deep breath through your nose, and then exhale through your mouth. Let's continue to live in God's love:

Psalm 118:24: "This is the day the Lord has made, and I will rejoice in it."

Psalm 119:165: "Great peace have they who love Your law; nothing shall offend them or make them stumble."

Psalm 120:7: "I am a man of peace."

Psalm 122:7: "May peace be within your walls and prosperity within your palaces."

Isaiah 66:12: "I will extend peace to her like a river."

Hebrews 12:14: "Make every effort to live in peace with all men."

2 Peter 1:2: "May grace and peace be multiplied to you in the knowledge of God and of Jesus our Lord."

Leviticus 26:6: "I will give peace in the land."

Relax, take a deep breath through your nose, and then exhale through your mouth. Let's continue to live in God's love:

Psalm 118:24: "This is the day the Lord has made, and I will rejoice in it."

You may open your eyes. Congratulate yourself! You have been given a new start in your life.

You will bring more positive energy to yourself and let more of God's love into your heart by listening to this Meditation and Prayer YDS CD over the next thirty days.

Thank you, and always remember that God is with you!

Just trust in Him!

(Reaffirm by beginning your Dear God Thankful Activity sheet)

Dear God,

I am so thankful for:

_____

_____

_____

_____

_____

_____

_____

_____

_____

_____

_____

_____

_____

_____

_____

_____

_____

_____

_____

_____

_____

_____

_____

_____

CHAPTER 10

LETTER TO GOD

A Moment with God

LETTER TO GOD

A Moment with God

Thank God for the things you are grateful for and the things He has provided for you. Think about the blessings you have received and thank Him for each one. Thank Him for a roof over your head, a job, the clothes on your back, food in your stomach. It's good to just put things in a positive viewpoint.

You can write Him any time you feel you want to. You can keep the letter in a drawer, hang it on your wall, or mail it. I believe His address is:

God
1 Sweet Street
Heaven, Universe 77777

Dear God,

I realize now that You were with me, God, during my hell. I truly believe that You allowed me to block certain events at the time they occurred in order to save me. I believe You permitted me to live two lives as a child: one in horror and shame, and the other in privilege. It was my privileged life that made me realize how good life can be.

I thank You, God, for giving me courage to have a voice.

I thank You, God, for allowing me to survive!

Humbly yours,
Yvette

Prayer Is Speaking to God. Meditation Is Listening to God.™

Dear God,

I want to *thank you* for:

_____

_____

_____

_____

_____

_____

_____

_____

_____

_____

_____

_____

_____

_____

_____

_____

_____

_____

_____

_____

_____

_____

_____

_____

_____

CHAPTER 11

LIFE LIST

Choices—Actions—Results

LIFE LIST

Choices—Actions—Results

This chapter is especially for you. Think about the things that you want to achieve and the changes you want to make in your life. Make promises to yourself—not to anyone else, but only you. Don't put limits on your list—such as money—by saying; "I can't afford it." Don't put time restraints on something by saying, "I don't have time or can't because of work, children, elderly parents, etc."

Put what you want to complete or achieve on your Life List as if there are no limitations. Write down a date by which you want to achieve it, change the date if you have to, and then check it off when you have accomplished this goal.

I began doing this in my early twenties. When I wanted to buy a new car, I test drove it and hung the brochure on my wall. Soon I was driving it. Another example was when I wanted to go to New York and Europe. I put a copy of a plane ticket, pictures of the places I wanted to see in my room and before I knew it, I was there. When I wanted a big fat savings account, I hung up deposit slips showing large deposits. You get the idea! People now call this process fulfilling their "bucket list." Call it what ever you want, just hang pictures of what you want to come to fruition without limits. Hang your list somewhere you can see it everyday. I think a Harry Winston diamond necklace would be just lovely.

Create your own morning and evening prayer. Think of a positive way you would like to start your day. Think of something you would like to end your day with.

Have fun with this.

Prayer Is Speaking to God. Meditation Is Listening to God.™

I Promise Myself

Write down the promises you want to make to yourself in your life:

I promise _____

I promise _____

I promise _____

I promise _____

I promise _____

I promise _____

I promise _____

I promise _____

I promise _____

I promise _____

I promise _____

I promise _____

I promise _____

I promise _____

I promise _____

I promise _____

I promise _____

I promise _____

I promise _____

I promise _____

LIFE LIST

☐ 1. _____

☐ 2. _____

☐ 3. _____

☐ 4. _____

☐ 5. _____

☐ 6. _____

☐ 7. _____

☐ 8. _____

☐ 9. _____

☐ 10. _____

☐ 11. _____

☐ 12. _____

☐ 13. _____

☐ 14. _____

☐ 15. _____

☐ 16. _____

☐ 17. _____

☐ 18. _____

☐ 19. _____

☐ 20. _____

☐ 21. _____

☐ 22. _____

☐ 23. _____

☐ 24. _____

☐ 25. _____

☐ 26. _____

☐ 27. _____

☐ 28. _____

☐ 29. _____

☐ 30. _____

☐ 31. _____

☐ 32. _____

☐ 33. _____

☐ 34. _____

☐ 35. _____

☐ 36. _____

☐ 37. _____

☐ 38. _____

☐ 39. _____

☐ 40. _____

☐ 41. _____

☐ 42. _____

☐ 43. _____

☐ 44. _____

☐ 45. _____

☐ 46. _____

☐ 47. _____

☐ 48. _____

☐ 49. _____

☐ 50. _____

☐ 51. _____

☐ 52. _____

☐ 53. _____

☐ 54. _____

☐ 55. _____

☐ 56. _____

☐ 57. _____

☐ 58. _____

☐ 59. _____

☐ 60. _____

☐ 61. _____

☐ 62. _____

☐ 63. _____

☐ 64. _____

☐ 65. _____

JOURNAL NOTES

JOURNAL NOTES

Journal Notes

_____

_____

_____

_____

_____

_____

_____

_____

_____

_____

_____

_____

_____

_____

_____

_____

_____

_____

_____

_____

_____

_____

_____

_____

_____

_____

JOURNAL NOTES

Journal Notes

JOURNAL NOTES

Journal Notes

CHAPTER 12

DAILY DIET

Your Body is a Temple

DAILY DIET

Your Body is a Temple

Dear Reader,

Let's be serious! You don't have to be a size zero or be magazine-model-thin, which is absurd. *That is not realistic.* This change is not about vanity. *It is about being healthy!* Eating fast foods and processed foods all the time does not have any nutritional value for your health, and will affect how you feel.

There are so many weight programs out there and I have been on several of them. Going further, I have also hired a Nutritionist, Marianne, to help me and my boys in this area. I thought I was doing a good job by buying foods that said, "healthy" or "real fruit juice." Then Marianne had me read the label, and I saw "10 percent juice." Next, she showed me how much sugar was actually in the "healthy" bars, granola bars, food in a box, etc. The so-called "natural" healthy foods had ingredients with words that I couldn't even pronounce.

Marianne explained what to look for and what to stay away from and it made sense. It was simple: *If it is man-made, think twice. If it is God-made, eat all you want.* Do your research and choose the diet program that best suits you. If you get bored, keep trying new things until you're healthy.

First, take inventory of what you are eating and add the calories. Make small modifications by reducing your calorie intake. Find one thing to change in your diet—but only one. Make this change for twenty-one days; then find another change. After twenty-one days, make another. Check with your doctor to determine your individual calorie intake.

To incorporate exercise into your daily health plan, do simple things, like park your car farther away from where you work, take long walks in the mall, take stairs instead of elevators, and dance to good music. Just start with one small change and add to it every twenty-one days.

Please don't get me wrong! I still carry around a few extra pounds that I would gladly give away, but I still love ice cream and pecan pie. Now, with the support of YDS, I eat them in moderation—and not every day.

If you slip up with your diet, just get back on track for the next meal. Don't think of your slip as blowing the whole day or your plans. For example, if you eat a donut for breakfast, be sure to have a salad or something healthy like that for lunch and dinner.

It takes twenty-one days to change a habit, but give yourself thirty days. *You are worth it!*

Disclaimer: Always consult your physician before you make any changes to your diet or begin any exercise regimen.

Prayer Is Speaking to God. Meditation Is Listening to God.™

DAILY DIET

Monday—Date _____   Total Oz. of Water _____   Total Calories _____

Breakfast _____   Calories _____

A.M. Snack _____   Calories _____

Lunch _____   Calories _____

P.M. Snack _____   Calories _____

Supper _____   Calories _____

Tuesday—Date_____   Total Oz. of Water_____   Total Calories _____

Breakfast _____   Calories _____

A.M. Snack _____   Calories _____

Lunch _____   Calories _____

P.M. Snack _____   Calories _____

Supper _____   Calories _____

Wednesday—Date _____   Total Oz. of Water _____   Total Calories _____

Breakfast _____   Calories _____

A.M. Snack _____   Calories _____

Lunch _____   Calories _____

P.M. Snack _____   Calories _____

Supper _____   Calories _____

Thursday—Date _____ Total Oz. of Water _____ Total Calories _____

Breakfast _____ Calories _____

A.M. Snack _____ Calories _____

Lunch _____ Calories _____

P.M. Snack _____ Calories _____

Supper _____ Calories _____

Friday—Date _____ Total Oz. of Water _____ Total Calories _____

Breakfast _____ Calories _____

A.M. Snack _____ Calories _____

Lunch _____ Calories _____

P.M. Snack _____ Calories _____

Supper _____ Calories _____

Saturday—Date _____ Total Oz. of Water _____ Total Calories _____

Breakfast _____ Calories _____

A.M. Snack _____ Calories _____

Lunch _____ Calories _____

P.M. Snack _____ Calories _____

Supper _____ Calories _____

Sunday—Date _____ Total Oz. of Water _____ Total Calories _____

Breakfast _____ Calories _____

A.M. Snack _____ Calories _____

Lunch _____ Calories _____

P.M. Snack _____ Calories _____

Supper _____ Calories _____

CHAPTER 13

HAPPY CARDS
AFFIRMATION CARDS
AND
SCRIPTURE CARDS

Tools and Resources

CARDS

Tools and Resources

Happy Cards: On the front side of each Happy Card, there is a positive scripture: "A happy heart is good medicine and a cheerful mind works healing." (Proverbs 17:22). If you see someone who needs a smile or needs to know someone else cares or just acknowledges that person's existence, let him or her know that everything will be okay and offer them a Happy Card or Just listen.

On the back side of each Happy Card, there is contact information about the Meditation & Prayer YDS LLC Program. If you know of or see someone who would benefit from the program, pass the card out to him or her. There are seven pages.

Affirmation Cards: These blank cards are for you to write the positive affirmations you have declared in the "I Am" and "Living in the Present" chapters all over your surroundings. You can choose your own or use positive quotes. Change them from time to time. There are seven pages.

Scripture Cards: The Scripture Affirmation Cards are longer. These blank cards are for you to put quotations from your favorite scriptures all over your surroundings. If you wish, you can use quotations from this workbook or choose your own from the Bible. Change them if you would like. There are seven pages.

Prayer Is Speaking to God. Meditation Is Listening to God.™

"A Happy Heart is
Good Medicine and a
Cheerful Mind Works Healing"

Proverb 17:22 AMP

"A Happy Heart is
Good Medicine and a
Cheerful Mind Works Healing"

Proverb 17:22 AMP

"A Happy Heart is
Good Medicine and a
Cheerful Mind Works Healing"

Proverb 17:22 AMP

"A Happy Heart is
Good Medicine and a
Cheerful Mind Works Healing"

Proverb 17:22 AMP

"A Happy Heart is
Good Medicine and a
Cheerful Mind Works Healing"

Proverb 17:22 AMP

"A Happy Heart is
Good Medicine and a
Cheerful Mind Works Healing"

Proverb 17:22 AMP

"A Happy Heart is
Good Medicine and a
Cheerful Mind Works Healing"

Proverb 17:22 AMP

"A Happy Heart is
Good Medicine and a
Cheerful Mind Works Healing"

Proverb 17:22 AMP

"A Happy Heart is
Good Medicine and a
Cheerful Mind Works Healing"

Proverb 17:22 AMP

"A Happy Heart is
Good Medicine and a
Cheerful Mind Works Healing"

Proverb 17:22 AMP

Meditation & Prayer YDS LLC

281-513-3614
www.mpyds.com
Facebook: Meditation & Prayer YDS

Meditation & Prayer YDS LLC

281-513-3614
www.mpyds.com
Facebook: Meditation & Prayer YDS

Meditation & Prayer YDS LLC

281-513-3614
www.mpyds.com
Facebook: Meditation & Prayer YDS

Meditation & Prayer YDS LLC

281-513-3614
www.mpyds.com
Facebook: Meditation & Prayer YDS

Meditation & Prayer YDS LLC

281-513-3614
www.mpyds.com
Facebook: Meditation & Prayer YDS

Meditation & Prayer YDS LLC

281-513-3614
www.mpyds.com
Facebook: Meditation & Prayer YDS

Meditation & Prayer YDS LLC

281-513-3614
www.mpyds.com
Facebook: Meditation & Prayer YDS

Meditation & Prayer YDS LLC

281-513-3614
www.mpyds.com
Facebook: Meditation & Prayer YDS

Meditation & Prayer YDS LLC

281-513-3614
www.mpyds.com
Facebook: Meditation & Prayer YDS

Meditation & Prayer YDS LLC

281-513-3614
www.mpyds.com
Facebook: Meditation & Prayer YDS

"A Happy Heart is
Good Medicine and a
Cheerful Mind Works Healing"

Proverb 17:22 AMP

"A Happy Heart is
Good Medicine and a
Cheerful Mind Works Healing"

Proverb 17:22 AMP

"A Happy Heart is
Good Medicine and a
Cheerful Mind Works Healing"

Proverb 17:22 AMP

"A Happy Heart is
Good Medicine and a
Cheerful Mind Works Healing"

Proverb 17:22 AMP

"A Happy Heart is
Good Medicine and a
Cheerful Mind Works Healing"

Proverb 17:22 AMP

"A Happy Heart is
Good Medicine and a
Cheerful Mind Works Healing"

Proverb 17:22 AMP

"A Happy Heart is
Good Medicine and a
Cheerful Mind Works Healing"

Proverb 17:22 AMP

"A Happy Heart is
Good Medicine and a
Cheerful Mind Works Healing"

Proverb 17:22 AMP

"A Happy Heart is
Good Medicine and a
Cheerful Mind Works Healing"

Proverb 17:22 AMP

"A Happy Heart is
Good Medicine and a
Cheerful Mind Works Healing"

Proverb 17:22 AMP

Meditation & Prayer YDS LLC 281-513-3614 www.mpyds.com Facebook: Meditation & Prayer YDS	**Meditation & Prayer YDS LLC** 281-513-3614 www.mpyds.com Facebook: Meditation & Prayer YDS
Meditation & Prayer YDS LLC 281-513-3614 www.mpyds.com Facebook: Meditation & Prayer YDS	**Meditation & Prayer YDS LLC** 281-513-3614 www.mpyds.com Facebook: Meditation & Prayer YDS
Meditation & Prayer YDS LLC 281-513-3614 www.mpyds.com Facebook: Meditation & Prayer YDS	**Meditation & Prayer YDS LLC** 281-513-3614 www.mpyds.com Facebook: Meditation & Prayer YDS
Meditation & Prayer YDS LLC 281-513-3614 www.mpyds.com Facebook: Meditation & Prayer YDS	**Meditation & Prayer YDS LLC** 281-513-3614 www.mpyds.com Facebook: Meditation & Prayer YDS
Meditation & Prayer YDS LLC 281-513-3614 www.mpyds.com Facebook: Meditation & Prayer YDS	**Meditation & Prayer YDS LLC** 281-513-3614 www.mpyds.com Facebook: Meditation & Prayer YDS

"A Happy Heart is
Good Medicine and a
Cheerful Mind Works Healing"

Proverb 17:22 AMP

"A Happy Heart is
Good Medicine and a
Cheerful Mind Works Healing"

Proverb 17:22 AMP

"A Happy Heart is
Good Medicine and a
Cheerful Mind Works Healing"

Proverb 17:22 AMP

"A Happy Heart is
Good Medicine and a
Cheerful Mind Works Healing"

Proverb 17:22 AMP

"A Happy Heart is
Good Medicine and a
Cheerful Mind Works Healing"

Proverb 17:22 AMP

"A Happy Heart is
Good Medicine and a
Cheerful Mind Works Healing"

Proverb 17:22 AMP

"A Happy Heart is
Good Medicine and a
Cheerful Mind Works Healing"

Proverb 17:22 AMP

"A Happy Heart is
Good Medicine and a
Cheerful Mind Works Healing"

Proverb 17:22 AMP

"A Happy Heart is
Good Medicine and a
Cheerful Mind Works Healing"

Proverb 17:22 AMP

"A Happy Heart is
Good Medicine and a
Cheerful Mind Works Healing"

Proverb 17:22 AMP

Meditation & Prayer YDS LLC

281-513-3614
www.mpyds.com
Facebook: Meditation & Prayer YDS

Meditation & Prayer YDS LLC

281-513-3614
www.mpyds.com
Facebook: Meditation & Prayer YDS

Meditation & Prayer YDS LLC

281-513-3614
www.mpyds.com
Facebook: Meditation & Prayer YDS

Meditation & Prayer YDS LLC

281-513-3614
www.mpyds.com
Facebook: Meditation & Prayer YDS

Meditation & Prayer YDS LLC

281-513-3614
www.mpyds.com
Facebook: Meditation & Prayer YDS

Meditation & Prayer YDS LLC

281-513-3614
www.mpyds.com
Facebook: Meditation & Prayer YDS

Meditation & Prayer YDS LLC

281-513-3614
www.mpyds.com
Facebook: Meditation & Prayer YDS

Meditation & Prayer YDS LLC

281-513-3614
www.mpyds.com
Facebook: Meditation & Prayer YDS

Meditation & Prayer YDS LLC

281-513-3614
www.mpyds.com
Facebook: Meditation & Prayer YDS

Meditation & Prayer YDS LLC

281-513-3614
www.mpyds.com
Facebook: Meditation & Prayer YDS

"A Happy Heart is
Good Medicine and a
Cheerful Mind Works Healing"

Proverb 17:22 AMP

"A Happy Heart is
Good Medicine and a
Cheerful Mind Works Healing"

Proverb 17:22 AMP

"A Happy Heart is
Good Medicine and a
Cheerful Mind Works Healing"

Proverb 17:22 AMP

"A Happy Heart is
Good Medicine and a
Cheerful Mind Works Healing"

Proverb 17:22 AMP

"A Happy Heart is
Good Medicine and a
Cheerful Mind Works Healing"

Proverb 17:22 AMP

"A Happy Heart is
Good Medicine and a
Cheerful Mind Works Healing"

Proverb 17:22 AMP

"A Happy Heart is
Good Medicine and a
Cheerful Mind Works Healing"

Proverb 17:22 AMP

"A Happy Heart is
Good Medicine and a
Cheerful Mind Works Healing"

Proverb 17:22 AMP

"A Happy Heart is
Good Medicine and a
Cheerful Mind Works Healing"

Proverb 17:22 AMP

"A Happy Heart is
Good Medicine and a
Cheerful Mind Works Healing"

Proverb 17:22 AMP

Meditation & Prayer YDS LLC	Meditation & Prayer YDS LLC
281-513-3614 www.mpyds.com Facebook: Meditation & Prayer YDS	281-513-3614 www.mpyds.com Facebook: Meditation & Prayer YDS
Meditation & Prayer YDS LLC	Meditation & Prayer YDS LLC
281-513-3614 www.mpyds.com Facebook: Meditation & Prayer YDS	281-513-3614 www.mpyds.com Facebook: Meditation & Prayer YDS
Meditation & Prayer YDS LLC	Meditation & Prayer YDS LLC
281-513-3614 www.mpyds.com Facebook: Meditation & Prayer YDS	281-513-3614 www.mpyds.com Facebook: Meditation & Prayer YDS
Meditation & Prayer YDS LLC	Meditation & Prayer YDS LLC
281-513-3614 www.mpyds.com Facebook: Meditation & Prayer YDS	281-513-3614 www.mpyds.com Facebook: Meditation & Prayer YDS
Meditation & Prayer YDS LLC	Meditation & Prayer YDS LLC
281-513-3614 www.mpyds.com Facebook: Meditation & Prayer YDS	281-513-3614 www.mpyds.com Facebook: Meditation & Prayer YDS

124

"A Happy Heart is
Good Medicine and a
Cheerful Mind Works Healing"

Proverb 17:22 AMP

"A Happy Heart is
Good Medicine and a
Cheerful Mind Works Healing"

Proverb 17:22 AMP

"A Happy Heart is
Good Medicine and a
Cheerful Mind Works Healing"

Proverb 17:22 AMP

"A Happy Heart is
Good Medicine and a
Cheerful Mind Works Healing"

Proverb 17:22 AMP

"A Happy Heart is
Good Medicine and a
Cheerful Mind Works Healing"

Proverb 17:22 AMP

"A Happy Heart is
Good Medicine and a
Cheerful Mind Works Healing"

Proverb 17:22 AMP

"A Happy Heart is
Good Medicine and a
Cheerful Mind Works Healing"

Proverb 17:22 AMP

"A Happy Heart is
Good Medicine and a
Cheerful Mind Works Healing"

Proverb 17:22 AMP

"A Happy Heart is
Good Medicine and a
Cheerful Mind Works Healing"

Proverb 17:22 AMP

"A Happy Heart is
Good Medicine and a
Cheerful Mind Works Healing"

Proverb 17:22 AMP

Meditation & Prayer YDS LLC 281-513-3614 www.mpyds.com Facebook: Meditation & Prayer YDS	**Meditation & Prayer YDS LLC** 281-513-3614 www.mpyds.com Facebook: Meditation & Prayer YDS
Meditation & Prayer YDS LLC 281-513-3614 www.mpyds.com Facebook: Meditation & Prayer YDS	**Meditation & Prayer YDS LLC** 281-513-3614 www.mpyds.com Facebook: Meditation & Prayer YDS
Meditation & Prayer YDS LLC 281-513-3614 www.mpyds.com Facebook: Meditation & Prayer YDS	**Meditation & Prayer YDS LLC** 281-513-3614 www.mpyds.com Facebook: Meditation & Prayer YDS
Meditation & Prayer YDS LLC 281-513-3614 www.mpyds.com Facebook: Meditation & Prayer YDS	**Meditation & Prayer YDS LLC** 281-513-3614 www.mpyds.com Facebook: Meditation & Prayer YDS
Meditation & Prayer YDS LLC 281-513-3614 www.mpyds.com Facebook: Meditation & Prayer YDS	**Meditation & Prayer YDS LLC** 281-513-3614 www.mpyds.com Facebook: Meditation & Prayer YDS

"A Happy Heart is
Good Medicine and a
Cheerful Mind Works Healing"

Proverb 17:22 AMP

"A Happy Heart is
Good Medicine and a
Cheerful Mind Works Healing"

Proverb 17:22 AMP

"A Happy Heart is
Good Medicine and a
Cheerful Mind Works Healing"

Proverb 17:22 AMP

"A Happy Heart is
Good Medicine and a
Cheerful Mind Works Healing"

Proverb 17:22 AMP

"A Happy Heart is
Good Medicine and a
Cheerful Mind Works Healing"

Proverb 17:22 AMP

"A Happy Heart is
Good Medicine and a
Cheerful Mind Works Healing"

Proverb 17:22 AMP

"A Happy Heart is
Good Medicine and a
Cheerful Mind Works Healing"

Proverb 17:22 AMP

"A Happy Heart is
Good Medicine and a
Cheerful Mind Works Healing"

Proverb 17:22 AMP

"A Happy Heart is
Good Medicine and a
Cheerful Mind Works Healing"

Proverb 17:22 AMP

"A Happy Heart is
Good Medicine and a
Cheerful Mind Works Healing"

Proverb 17:22 AMP

Meditation & Prayer YDS LLC

281-513-3614
www.mpyds.com
Facebook: Meditation & Prayer YDS

Meditation & Prayer YDS LLC

281-513-3614
www.mpyds.com
Facebook: Meditation & Prayer YDS

Meditation & Prayer YDS LLC

281-513-3614
www.mpyds.com
Facebook: Meditation & Prayer YDS

Meditation & Prayer YDS LLC

281-513-3614
www.mpyds.com
Facebook: Meditation & Prayer YDS

Meditation & Prayer YDS LLC

281-513-3614
www.mpyds.com
Facebook: Meditation & Prayer YDS

Meditation & Prayer YDS LLC

281-513-3614
www.mpyds.com
Facebook: Meditation & Prayer YDS

Meditation & Prayer YDS LLC

281-513-3614
www.mpyds.com
Facebook: Meditation & Prayer YDS

Meditation & Prayer YDS LLC

281-513-3614
www.mpyds.com
Facebook: Meditation & Prayer YDS

Meditation & Prayer YDS LLC

281-513-3614
www.mpyds.com
Facebook: Meditation & Prayer YDS

Meditation & Prayer YDS LLC

281-513-3614
www.mpyds.com
Facebook: Meditation & Prayer YDS

"A Happy Heart is
Good Medicine and a
Cheerful Mind Works Healing"

Proverb 17:22 AMP

"A Happy Heart is
Good Medicine and a
Cheerful Mind Works Healing"

Proverb 17:22 AMP

"A Happy Heart is
Good Medicine and a
Cheerful Mind Works Healing"

Proverb 17:22 AMP

"A Happy Heart is
Good Medicine and a
Cheerful Mind Works Healing"

Proverb 17:22 AMP

"A Happy Heart is
Good Medicine and a
Cheerful Mind Works Healing"

Proverb 17:22 AMP

"A Happy Heart is
Good Medicine and a
Cheerful Mind Works Healing"

Proverb 17:22 AMP

"A Happy Heart is
Good Medicine and a
Cheerful Mind Works Healing"

Proverb 17:22 AMP

"A Happy Heart is
Good Medicine and a
Cheerful Mind Works Healing"

Proverb 17:22 AMP

"A Happy Heart is
Good Medicine and a
Cheerful Mind Works Healing"

Proverb 17:22 AMP

"A Happy Heart is
Good Medicine and a
Cheerful Mind Works Healing"

Proverb 17:22 AMP

129

Meditation & Prayer YDS LLC

281-513-3614
www.mpyds.com
Facebook: Meditation & Prayer YDS

Meditation & Prayer YDS LLC

281-513-3614
www.mpyds.com
Facebook: Meditation & Prayer YDS

Meditation & Prayer YDS LLC

281-513-3614
www.mpyds.com
Facebook: Meditation & Prayer YDS

Meditation & Prayer YDS LLC

281-513-3614
www.mpyds.com
Facebook: Meditation & Prayer YDS

Meditation & Prayer YDS LLC

281-513-3614
www.mpyds.com
Facebook: Meditation & Prayer YDS

Meditation & Prayer YDS LLC

281-513-3614
www.mpyds.com
Facebook: Meditation & Prayer YDS

Meditation & Prayer YDS LLC

281-513-3614
www.mpyds.com
Facebook: Meditation & Prayer YDS

Meditation & Prayer YDS LLC

281-513-3614
www.mpyds.com
Facebook: Meditation & Prayer YDS

Meditation & Prayer YDS LLC

281-513-3614
www.mpyds.com
Facebook: Meditation & Prayer YDS

Meditation & Prayer YDS LLC

281-513-3614
www.mpyds.com
Facebook: Meditation & Prayer YDS

"A Happy Heart is
Good Medicine and a
Cheerful Mind Works Healing"

Proverb 17:22 AMP

"A Happy Heart is
Good Medicine and a
Cheerful Mind Works Healing"

Proverb 17:22 AMP

"A Happy Heart is
Good Medicine and a
Cheerful Mind Works Healing"

Proverb 17:22 AMP

"A Happy Heart is
Good Medicine and a
Cheerful Mind Works Healing"

Proverb 17:22 AMP

"A Happy Heart is
Good Medicine and a
Cheerful Mind Works Healing"

Proverb 17:22 AMP

"A Happy Heart is
Good Medicine and a
Cheerful Mind Works Healing"

Proverb 17:22 AMP

"A Happy Heart is
Good Medicine and a
Cheerful Mind Works Healing"

Proverb 17:22 AMP

"A Happy Heart is
Good Medicine and a
Cheerful Mind Works Healing"

Proverb 17:22 AMP

"A Happy Heart is
Good Medicine and a
Cheerful Mind Works Healing"

Proverb 17:22 AMP

"A Happy Heart is
Good Medicine and a
Cheerful Mind Works Healing"

Proverb 17:22 AMP

Meditation & Prayer YDS LLC	Meditation & Prayer YDS LLC
281-513-3614 www.mpyds.com Facebook: Meditation & Prayer YDS	281-513-3614 www.mpyds.com Facebook: Meditation & Prayer YDS
Meditation & Prayer YDS LLC	Meditation & Prayer YDS LLC
281-513-3614 www.mpyds.com Facebook: Meditation & Prayer YDS	281-513-3614 www.mpyds.com Facebook: Meditation & Prayer YDS
Meditation & Prayer YDS LLC	Meditation & Prayer YDS LLC
281-513-3614 www.mpyds.com Facebook: Meditation & Prayer YDS	281-513-3614 www.mpyds.com Facebook: Meditation & Prayer YDS
Meditation & Prayer YDS LLC	Meditation & Prayer YDS LLC
281-513-3614 www.mpyds.com Facebook: Meditation & Prayer YDS	281-513-3614 www.mpyds.com Facebook: Meditation & Prayer YDS
Meditation & Prayer YDS LLC	Meditation & Prayer YDS LLC
281-513-3614 www.mpyds.com Facebook: Meditation & Prayer YDS	281-513-3614 www.mpyds.com Facebook: Meditation & Prayer YDS

"A Happy Heart is
Good Medicine and a
Cheerful Mind Works Healing"

Proverb 17:22 AMP

"A Happy Heart is
Good Medicine and a
Cheerful Mind Works Healing"

Proverb 17:22 AMP

"A Happy Heart is
Good Medicine and a
Cheerful Mind Works Healing"

Proverb 17:22 AMP

"A Happy Heart is
Good Medicine and a
Cheerful Mind Works Healing"

Proverb 17:22 AMP

"A Happy Heart is
Good Medicine and a
Cheerful Mind Works Healing"

Proverb 17:22 AMP

"A Happy Heart is
Good Medicine and a
Cheerful Mind Works Healing"

Proverb 17:22 AMP

"A Happy Heart is
Good Medicine and a
Cheerful Mind Works Healing"

Proverb 17:22 AMP

"A Happy Heart is
Good Medicine and a
Cheerful Mind Works Healing"

Proverb 17:22 AMP

"A Happy Heart is
Good Medicine and a
Cheerful Mind Works Healing"

Proverb 17:22 AMP

"A Happy Heart is
Good Medicine and a
Cheerful Mind Works Healing"

Proverb 17:22 AMP

Meditation & Prayer YDS LLC	Meditation & Prayer YDS LLC
281-513-3614 www.mpyds.com Facebook: Meditation & Prayer YDS	281-513-3614 www.mpyds.com Facebook: Meditation & Prayer YDS
Meditation & Prayer YDS LLC	Meditation & Prayer YDS LLC
281-513-3614 www.mpyds.com Facebook: Meditation & Prayer YDS	281-513-3614 www.mpyds.com Facebook: Meditation & Prayer YDS
Meditation & Prayer YDS LLC	Meditation & Prayer YDS LLC
281-513-3614 www.mpyds.com Facebook: Meditation & Prayer YDS	281-513-3614 www.mpyds.com Facebook: Meditation & Prayer YDS
Meditation & Prayer YDS LLC	Meditation & Prayer YDS LLC
281-513-3614 www.mpyds.com Facebook: Meditation & Prayer YDS	281-513-3614 www.mpyds.com Facebook: Meditation & Prayer YDS
Meditation & Prayer YDS LLC	Meditation & Prayer YDS LLC
281-513-3614 www.mpyds.com Facebook: Meditation & Prayer YDS	281-513-3614 www.mpyds.com Facebook: Meditation & Prayer YDS

"A Happy Heart is
Good Medicine and a
Cheerful Mind Works Healing"

Proverb 17:22 AMP

"A Happy Heart is
Good Medicine and a
Cheerful Mind Works Healing"

Proverb 17:22 AMP

"A Happy Heart is
Good Medicine and a
Cheerful Mind Works Healing"

Proverb 17:22 AMP

"A Happy Heart is
Good Medicine and a
Cheerful Mind Works Healing"

Proverb 17:22 AMP

"A Happy Heart is
Good Medicine and a
Cheerful Mind Works Healing"

Proverb 17:22 AMP

"A Happy Heart is
Good Medicine and a
Cheerful Mind Works Healing"

Proverb 17:22 AMP

"A Happy Heart is
Good Medicine and a
Cheerful Mind Works Healing"

Proverb 17:22 AMP

"A Happy Heart is
Good Medicine and a
Cheerful Mind Works Healing"

Proverb 17:22 AMP

"A Happy Heart is
Good Medicine and a
Cheerful Mind Works Healing"

Proverb 17:22 AMP

"A Happy Heart is
Good Medicine and a
Cheerful Mind Works Healing"

Proverb 17:22 AMP

Meditation & Prayer YDS LLC

281-513-3614
www.mpyds.com
Facebook: Meditation & Prayer YDS

Meditation & Prayer YDS LLC

281-513-3614
www.mpyds.com
Facebook: Meditation & Prayer YDS

Meditation & Prayer YDS LLC

281-513-3614
www.mpyds.com
Facebook: Meditation & Prayer YDS

Meditation & Prayer YDS LLC

281-513-3614
www.mpyds.com
Facebook: Meditation & Prayer YDS

Meditation & Prayer YDS LLC

281-513-3614
www.mpyds.com
Facebook: Meditation & Prayer YDS

Meditation & Prayer YDS LLC

281-513-3614
www.mpyds.com
Facebook: Meditation & Prayer YDS

Meditation & Prayer YDS LLC

281-513-3614
www.mpyds.com
Facebook: Meditation & Prayer YDS

Meditation & Prayer YDS LLC

281-513-3614
www.mpyds.com
Facebook: Meditation & Prayer YDS

Meditation & Prayer YDS LLC

281-513-3614
www.mpyds.com
Facebook: Meditation & Prayer YDS

Meditation & Prayer YDS LLC

281-513-3614
www.mpyds.com
Facebook: Meditation & Prayer YDS

"A Happy Heart is
Good Medicine and a
Cheerful Mind Works Healing"

Proverb 17:22 AMP

"A Happy Heart is
Good Medicine and a
Cheerful Mind Works Healing"

Proverb 17:22 AMP

"A Happy Heart is
Good Medicine and a
Cheerful Mind Works Healing"

Proverb 17:22 AMP

"A Happy Heart is
Good Medicine and a
Cheerful Mind Works Healing"

Proverb 17:22 AMP

"A Happy Heart is
Good Medicine and a
Cheerful Mind Works Healing"

Proverb 17:22 AMP

"A Happy Heart is
Good Medicine and a
Cheerful Mind Works Healing"

Proverb 17:22 AMP

"A Happy Heart is
Good Medicine and a
Cheerful Mind Works Healing"

Proverb 17:22 AMP

"A Happy Heart is
Good Medicine and a
Cheerful Mind Works Healing"

Proverb 17:22 AMP

"A Happy Heart is
Good Medicine and a
Cheerful Mind Works Healing"

Proverb 17:22 AMP

"A Happy Heart is
Good Medicine and a
Cheerful Mind Works Healing"

Proverb 17:22 AMP

Meditation & Prayer YDS LLC 281-513-3614 www.mpyds.com Facebook: Meditation & Prayer YDS	**Meditation & Prayer YDS LLC** 281-513-3614 www.mpyds.com Facebook: Meditation & Prayer YDS
Meditation & Prayer YDS LLC 281-513-3614 www.mpyds.com Facebook: Meditation & Prayer YDS	**Meditation & Prayer YDS LLC** 281-513-3614 www.mpyds.com Facebook: Meditation & Prayer YDS
Meditation & Prayer YDS LLC 281-513-3614 www.mpyds.com Facebook: Meditation & Prayer YDS	**Meditation & Prayer YDS LLC** 281-513-3614 www.mpyds.com Facebook: Meditation & Prayer YDS
Meditation & Prayer YDS LLC 281-513-3614 www.mpyds.com Facebook: Meditation & Prayer YDS	**Meditation & Prayer YDS LLC** 281-513-3614 www.mpyds.com Facebook: Meditation & Prayer YDS
Meditation & Prayer YDS LLC 281-513-3614 www.mpyds.com Facebook: Meditation & Prayer YDS	**Meditation & Prayer YDS LLC** 281-513-3614 www.mpyds.com Facebook: Meditation & Prayer YDS

"A Happy Heart is
Good Medicine and a
Cheerful Mind Works Healing"

Proverb 17:22 AMP

"A Happy Heart is
Good Medicine and a
Cheerful Mind Works Healing"

Proverb 17:22 AMP

"A Happy Heart is
Good Medicine and a
Cheerful Mind Works Healing"

Proverb 17:22 AMP

"A Happy Heart is
Good Medicine and a
Cheerful Mind Works Healing"

Proverb 17:22 AMP

"A Happy Heart is
Good Medicine and a
Cheerful Mind Works Healing"

Proverb 17:22 AMP

"A Happy Heart is
Good Medicine and a
Cheerful Mind Works Healing"

Proverb 17:22 AMP

"A Happy Heart is
Good Medicine and a
Cheerful Mind Works Healing"

Proverb 17:22 AMP

"A Happy Heart is
Good Medicine and a
Cheerful Mind Works Healing"

Proverb 17:22 AMP

"A Happy Heart is
Good Medicine and a
Cheerful Mind Works Healing"

Proverb 17:22 AMP

"A Happy Heart is
Good Medicine and a
Cheerful Mind Works Healing"

Proverb 17:22 AMP

Meditation & Prayer YDS LLC 281-513-3614 www.mpyds.com Facebook: Meditation & Prayer YDS	**Meditation & Prayer YDS LLC** 281-513-3614 www.mpyds.com Facebook: Meditation & Prayer YDS
Meditation & Prayer YDS LLC 281-513-3614 www.mpyds.com Facebook: Meditation & Prayer YDS	**Meditation & Prayer YDS LLC** 281-513-3614 www.mpyds.com Facebook: Meditation & Prayer YDS
Meditation & Prayer YDS LLC 281-513-3614 www.mpyds.com Facebook: Meditation & Prayer YDS	**Meditation & Prayer YDS LLC** 281-513-3614 www.mpyds.com Facebook: Meditation & Prayer YDS
Meditation & Prayer YDS LLC 281-513-3614 www.mpyds.com Facebook: Meditation & Prayer YDS	**Meditation & Prayer YDS LLC** 281-513-3614 www.mpyds.com Facebook: Meditation & Prayer YDS
Meditation & Prayer YDS LLC 281-513-3614 www.mpyds.com Facebook: Meditation & Prayer YDS	**Meditation & Prayer YDS LLC** 281-513-3614 www.mpyds.com Facebook: Meditation & Prayer YDS

"A Happy Heart is
Good Medicine and a
Cheerful Mind Works Healing"

Proverb 17:22 AMP

"A Happy Heart is
Good Medicine and a
Cheerful Mind Works Healing"

Proverb 17:22 AMP

"A Happy Heart is
Good Medicine and a
Cheerful Mind Works Healing"

Proverb 17:22 AMP

"A Happy Heart is
Good Medicine and a
Cheerful Mind Works Healing"

Proverb 17:22 AMP

"A Happy Heart is
Good Medicine and a
Cheerful Mind Works Healing"

Proverb 17:22 AMP

"A Happy Heart is
Good Medicine and a
Cheerful Mind Works Healing"

Proverb 17:22 AMP

"A Happy Heart is
Good Medicine and a
Cheerful Mind Works Healing"

Proverb 17:22 AMP

"A Happy Heart is
Good Medicine and a
Cheerful Mind Works Healing"

Proverb 17:22 AMP

"A Happy Heart is
Good Medicine and a
Cheerful Mind Works Healing"

Proverb 17:22 AMP

"A Happy Heart is
Good Medicine and a
Cheerful Mind Works Healing"

Proverb 17:22 AMP

Meditation & Prayer YDS LLC

281-513-3614
www.mpyds.com
Facebook: Meditation & Prayer YDS

Meditation & Prayer YDS LLC

281-513-3614
www.mpyds.com
Facebook: Meditation & Prayer YDS

Meditation & Prayer YDS LLC

281-513-3614
www.mpyds.com
Facebook: Meditation & Prayer YDS

Meditation & Prayer YDS LLC

281-513-3614
www.mpyds.com
Facebook: Meditation & Prayer YDS

Meditation & Prayer YDS LLC

281-513-3614
www.mpyds.com
Facebook: Meditation & Prayer YDS

Meditation & Prayer YDS LLC

281-513-3614
www.mpyds.com
Facebook: Meditation & Prayer YDS

Meditation & Prayer YDS LLC

281-513-3614
www.mpyds.com
Facebook: Meditation & Prayer YDS

Meditation & Prayer YDS LLC

281-513-3614
www.mpyds.com
Facebook: Meditation & Prayer YDS

Meditation & Prayer YDS LLC

281-513-3614
www.mpyds.com
Facebook: Meditation & Prayer YDS

Meditation & Prayer YDS LLC

281-513-3614
www.mpyds.com
Facebook: Meditation & Prayer YDS

"A Happy Heart is
Good Medicine and a
Cheerful Mind Works Healing"

Proverb 17:22 AMP

"A Happy Heart is
Good Medicine and a
Cheerful Mind Works Healing"

Proverb 17:22 AMP

"A Happy Heart is
Good Medicine and a
Cheerful Mind Works Healing"

Proverb 17:22 AMP

"A Happy Heart is
Good Medicine and a
Cheerful Mind Works Healing"

Proverb 17:22 AMP

"A Happy Heart is
Good Medicine and a
Cheerful Mind Works Healing"

Proverb 17:22 AMP

"A Happy Heart is
Good Medicine and a
Cheerful Mind Works Healing"

Proverb 17:22 AMP

"A Happy Heart is
Good Medicine and a
Cheerful Mind Works Healing"

Proverb 17:22 AMP

"A Happy Heart is
Good Medicine and a
Cheerful Mind Works Healing"

Proverb 17:22 AMP

"A Happy Heart is
Good Medicine and a
Cheerful Mind Works Healing"

Proverb 17:22 AMP

"A Happy Heart is
Good Medicine and a
Cheerful Mind Works Healing"

Proverb 17:22 AMP

Meditation & Prayer YDS LLC

281-513-3614
www.mpyds.com
Facebook: Meditation & Prayer YDS

Meditation & Prayer YDS LLC

281-513-3614
www.mpyds.com
Facebook: Meditation & Prayer YDS

Meditation & Prayer YDS LLC

281-513-3614
www.mpyds.com
Facebook: Meditation & Prayer YDS

Meditation & Prayer YDS LLC

281-513-3614
www.mpyds.com
Facebook: Meditation & Prayer YDS

Meditation & Prayer YDS LLC

281-513-3614
www.mpyds.com
Facebook: Meditation & Prayer YDS

Meditation & Prayer YDS LLC

281-513-3614
www.mpyds.com
Facebook: Meditation & Prayer YDS

Meditation & Prayer YDS LLC

281-513-3614
www.mpyds.com
Facebook: Meditation & Prayer YDS

Meditation & Prayer YDS LLC

281-513-3614
www.mpyds.com
Facebook: Meditation & Prayer YDS

Meditation & Prayer YDS LLC

281-513-3614
www.mpyds.com
Facebook: Meditation & Prayer YDS

Meditation & Prayer YDS LLC

281-513-3614
www.mpyds.com
Facebook: Meditation & Prayer YDS

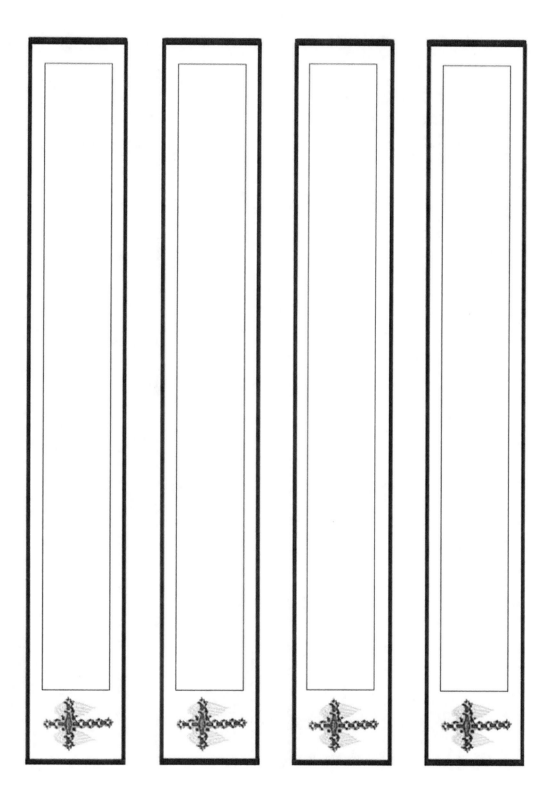

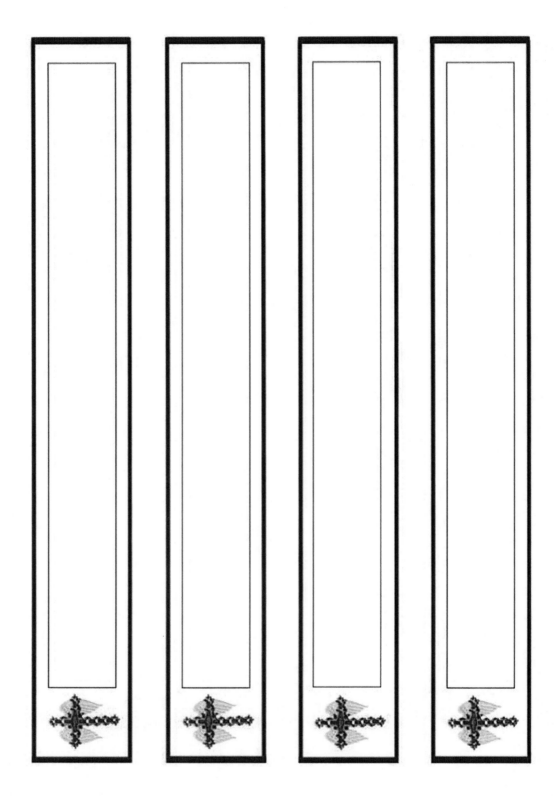

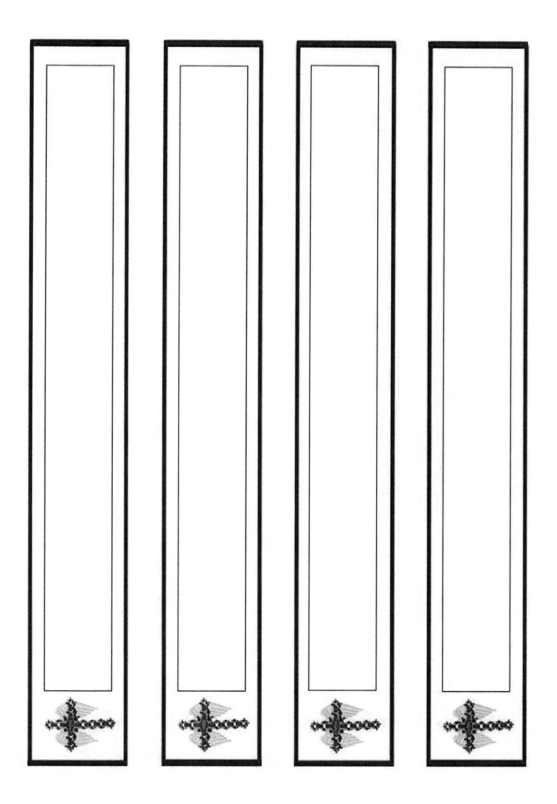

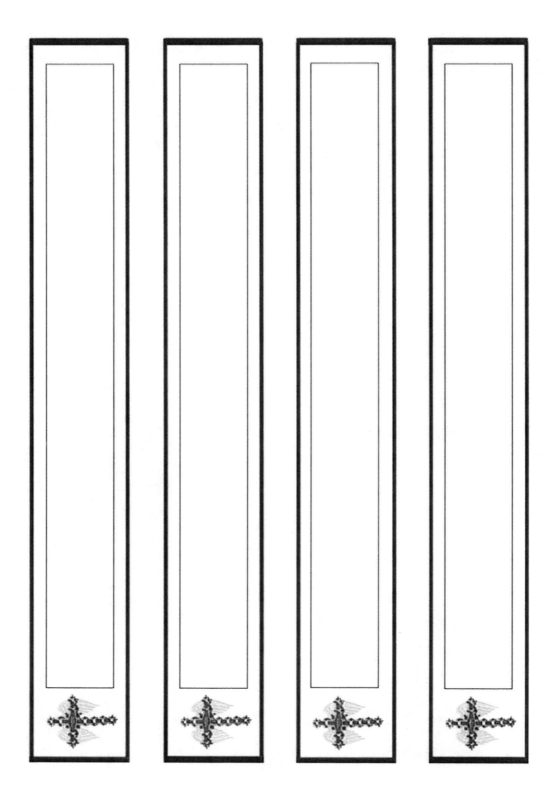

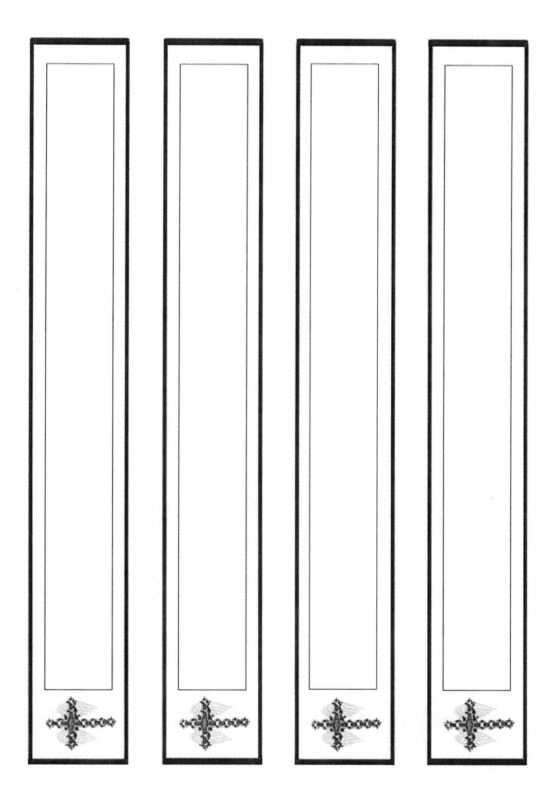

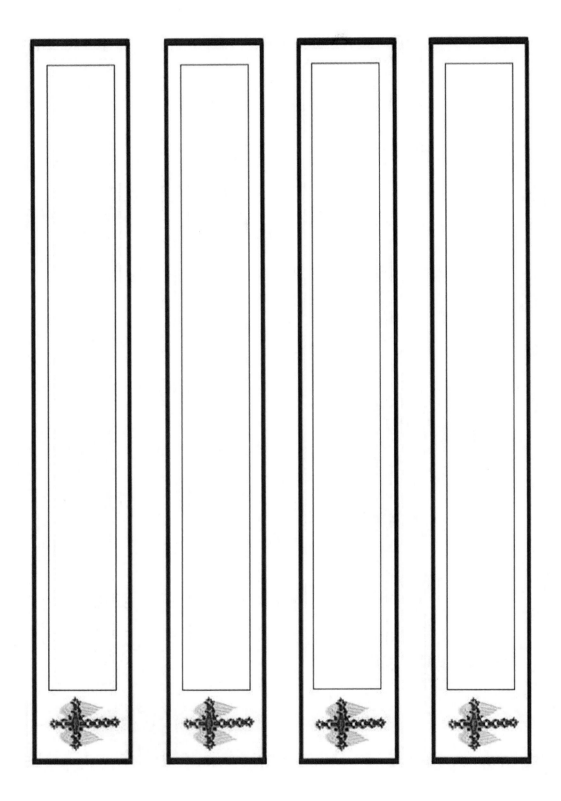

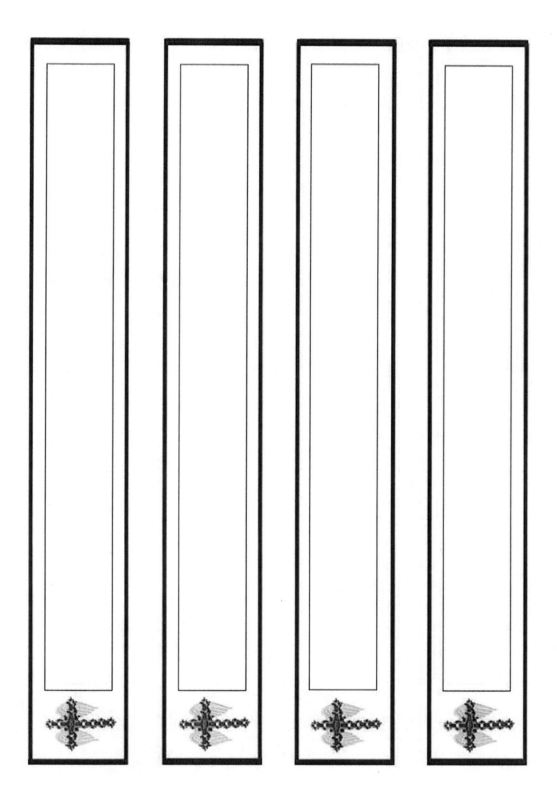

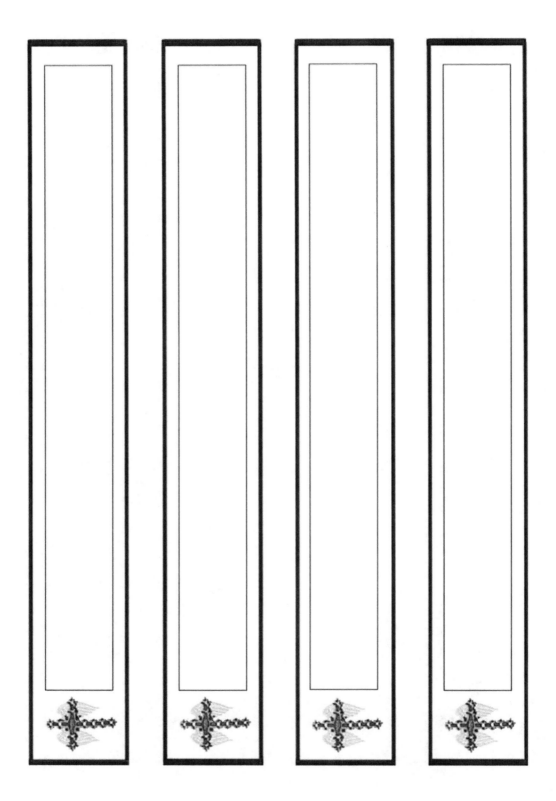

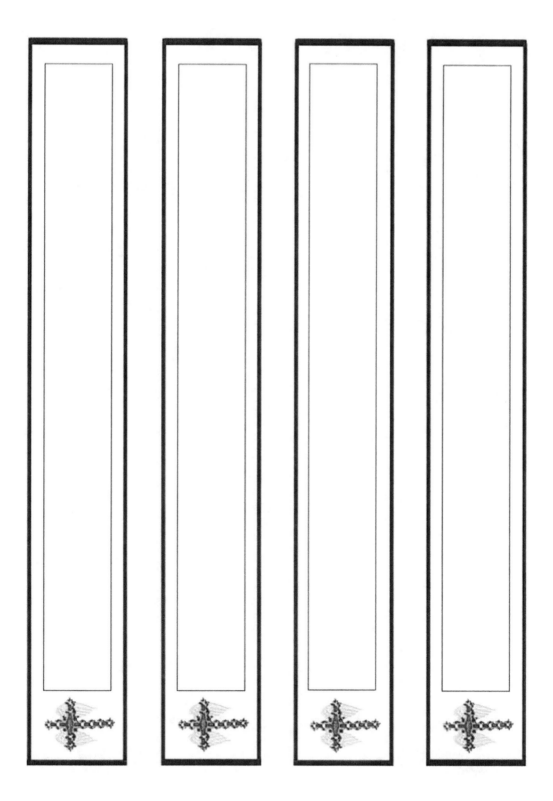

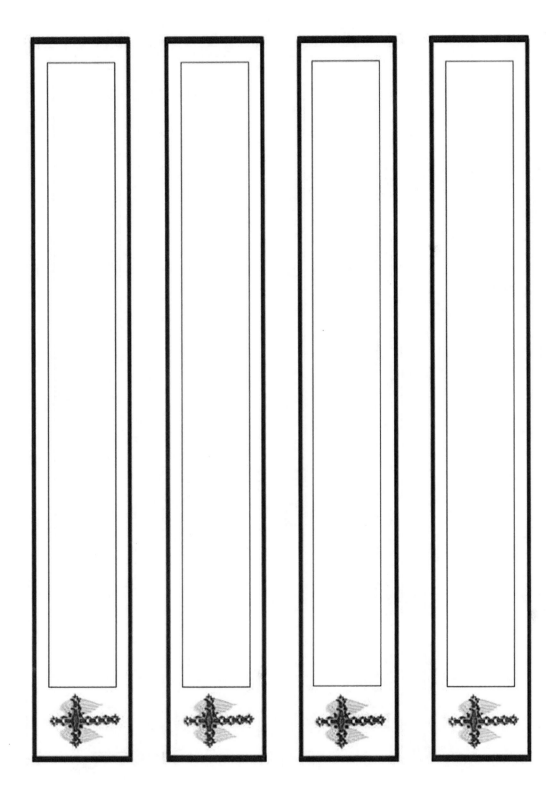

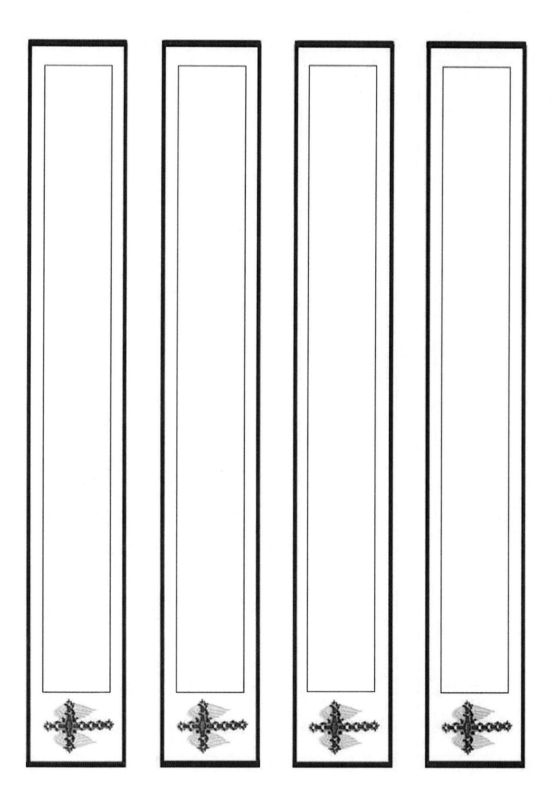

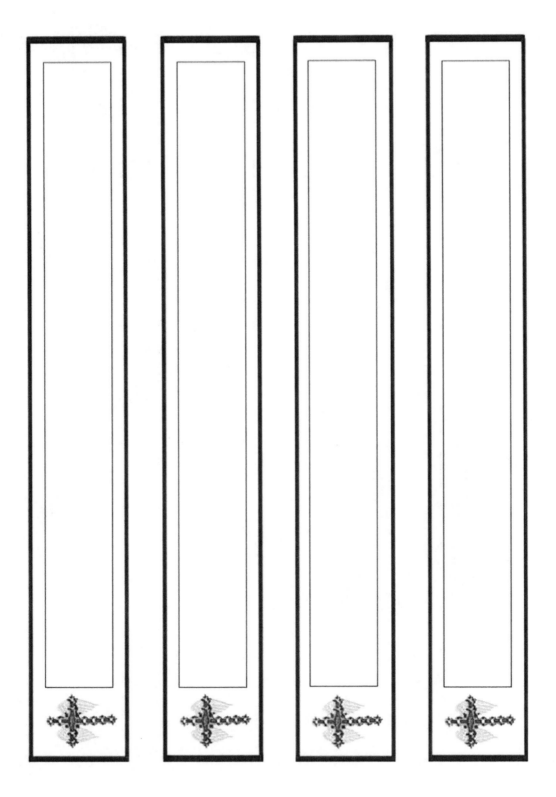

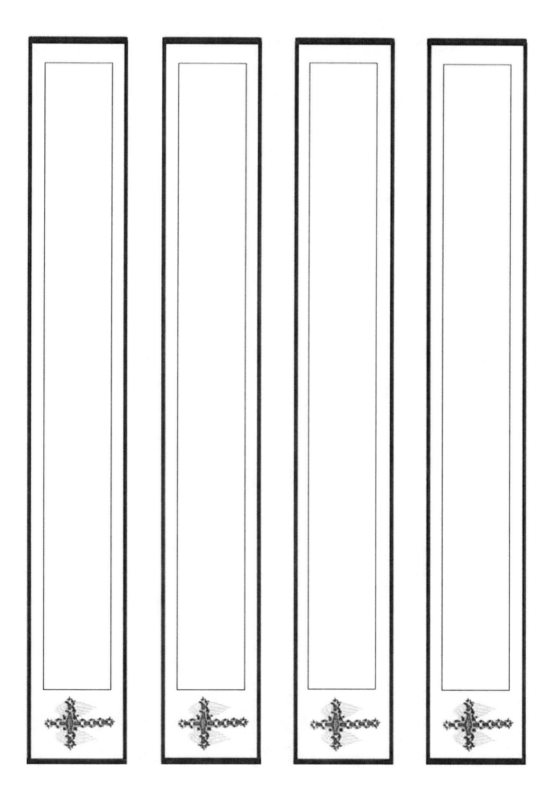

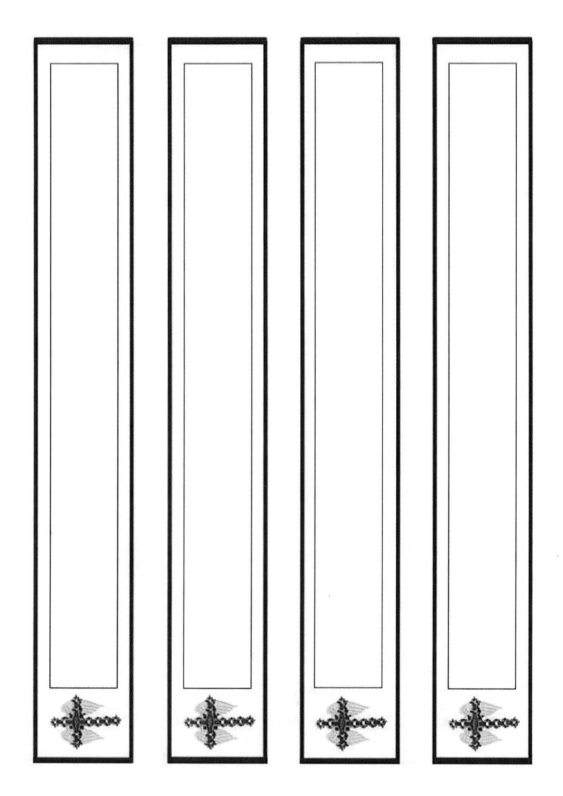

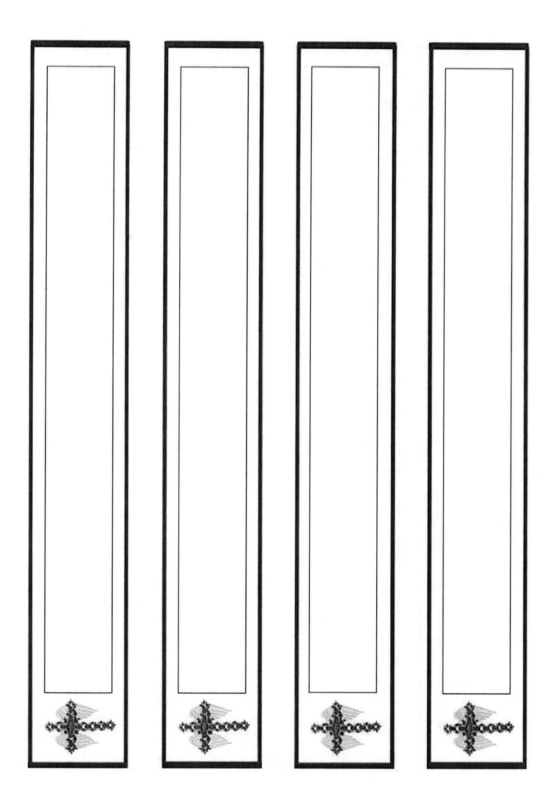

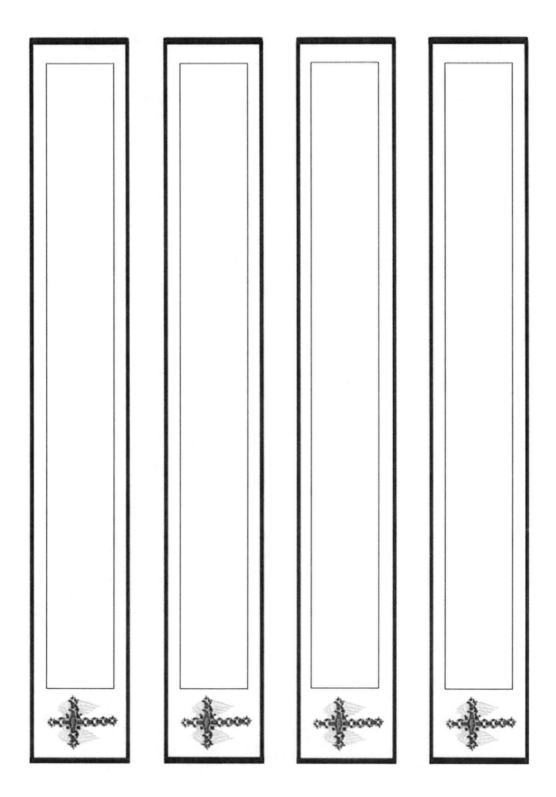

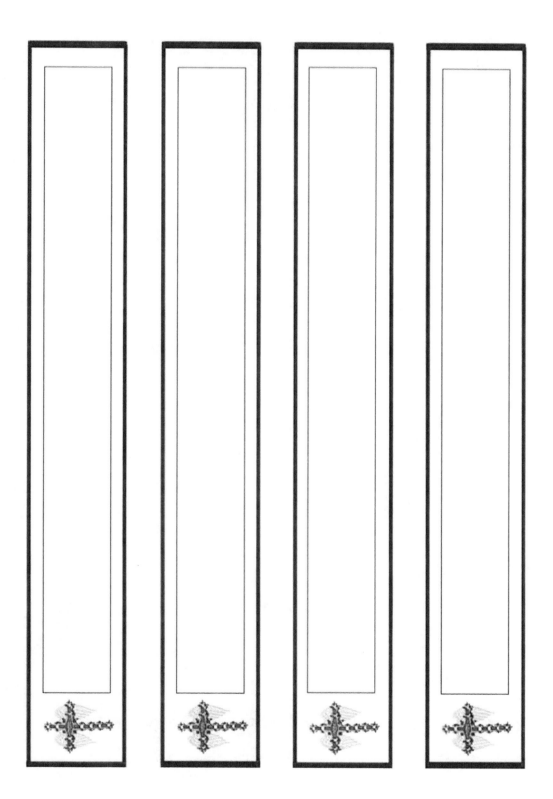

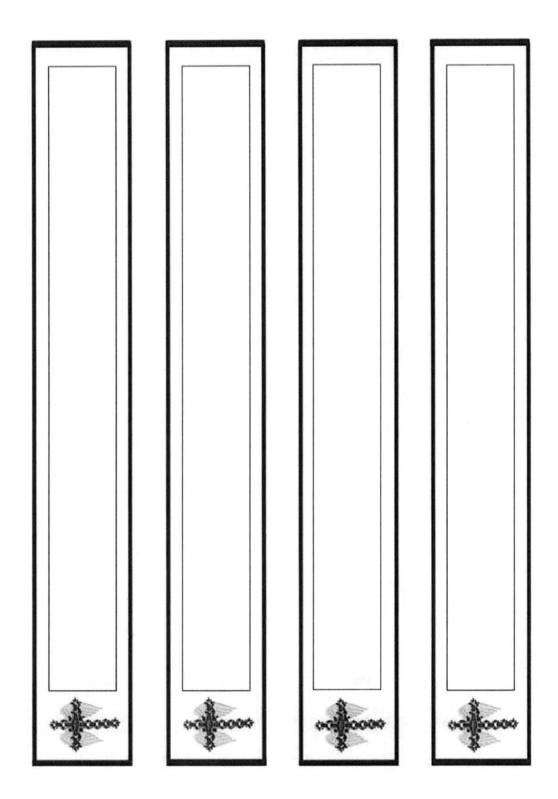

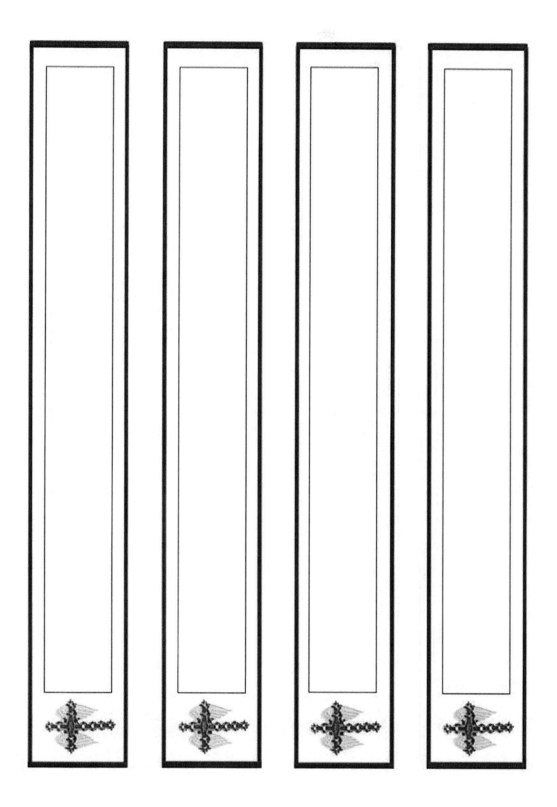

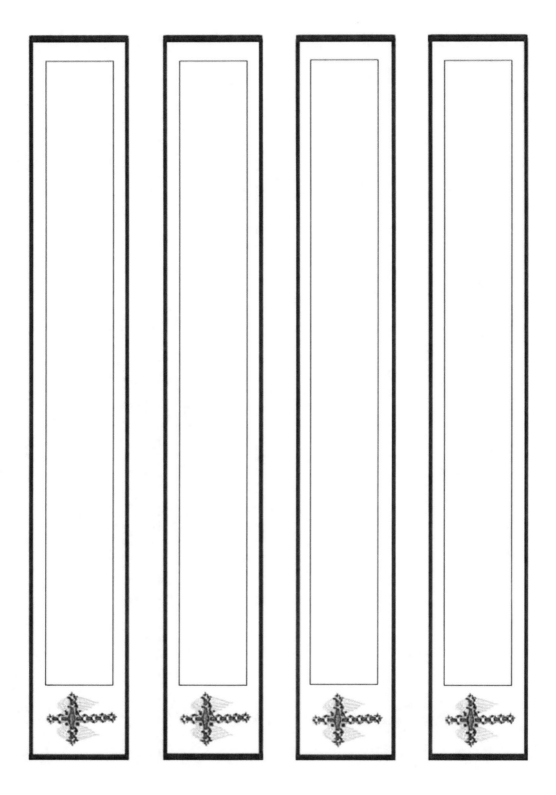

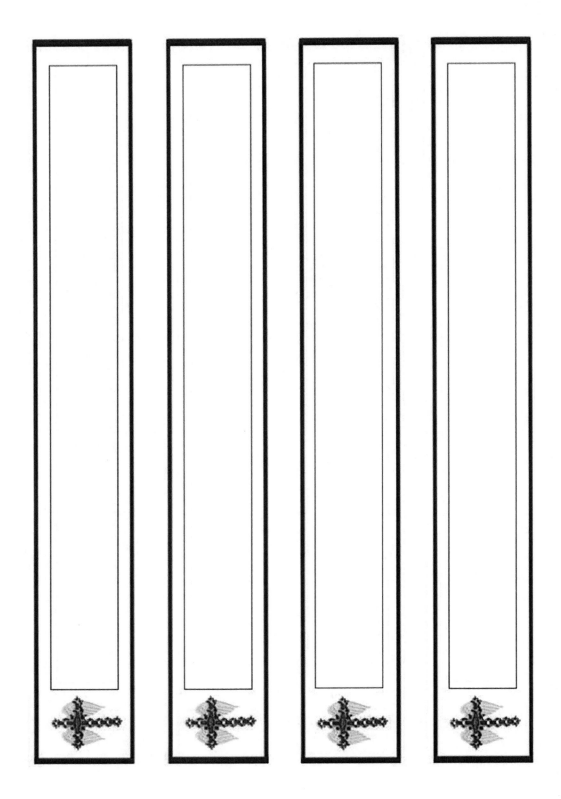

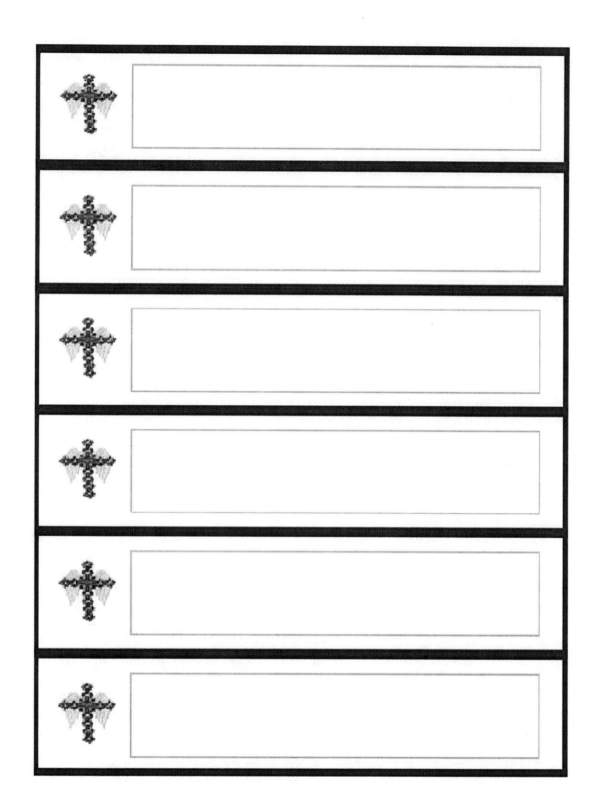

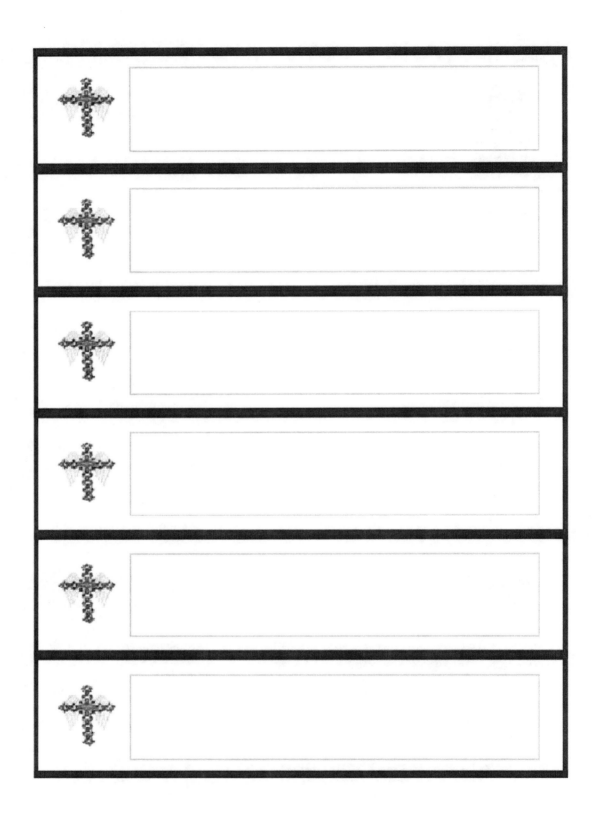

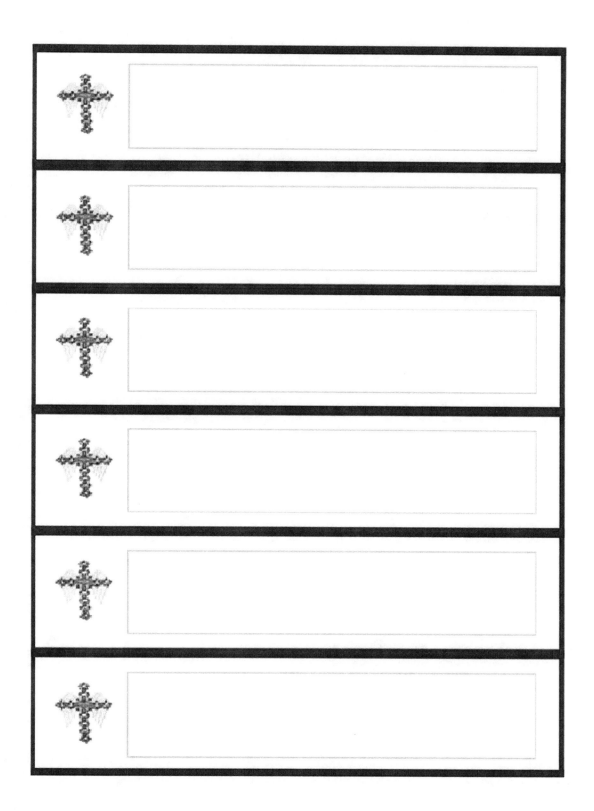

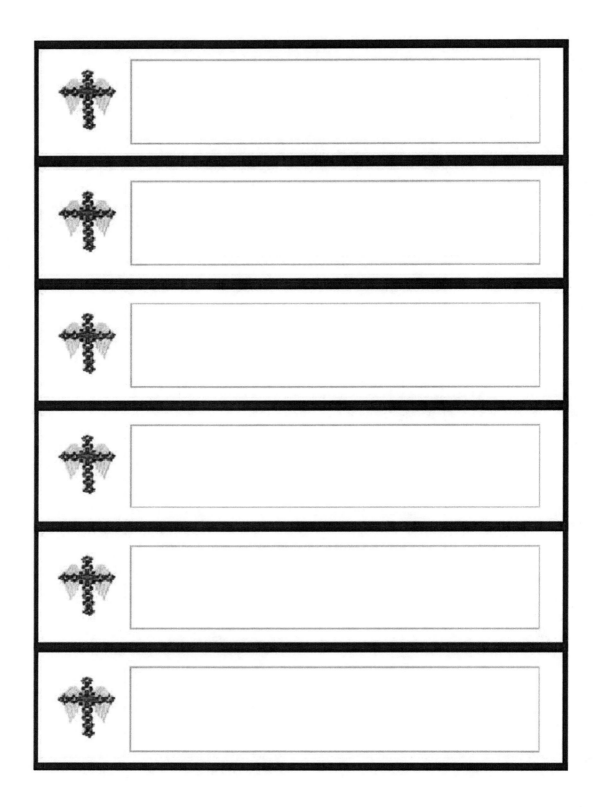

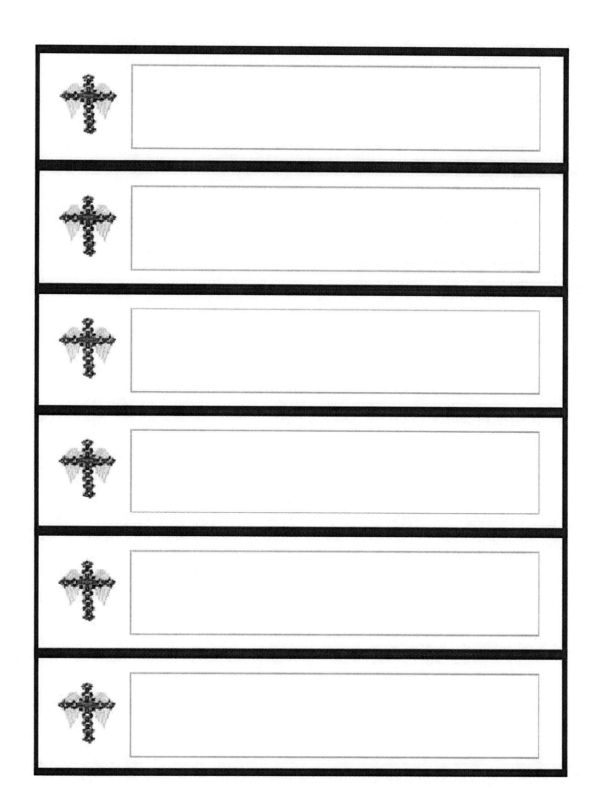

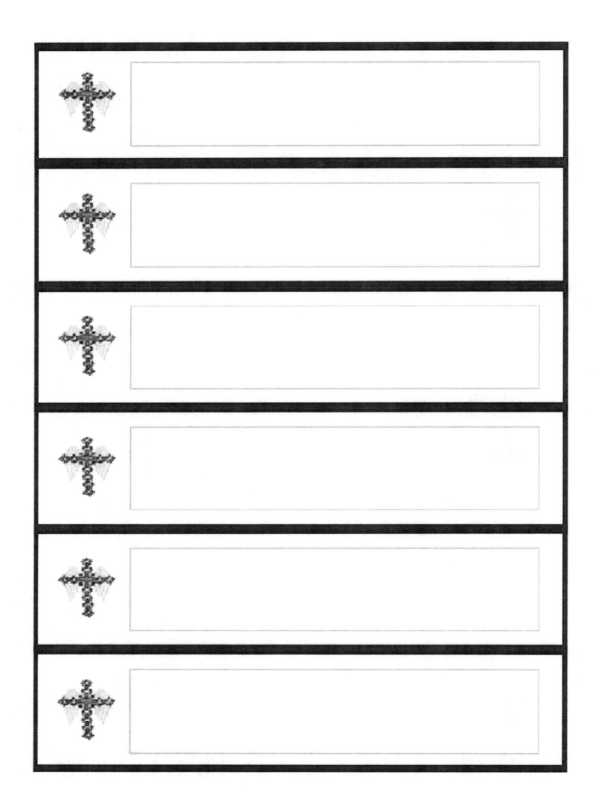

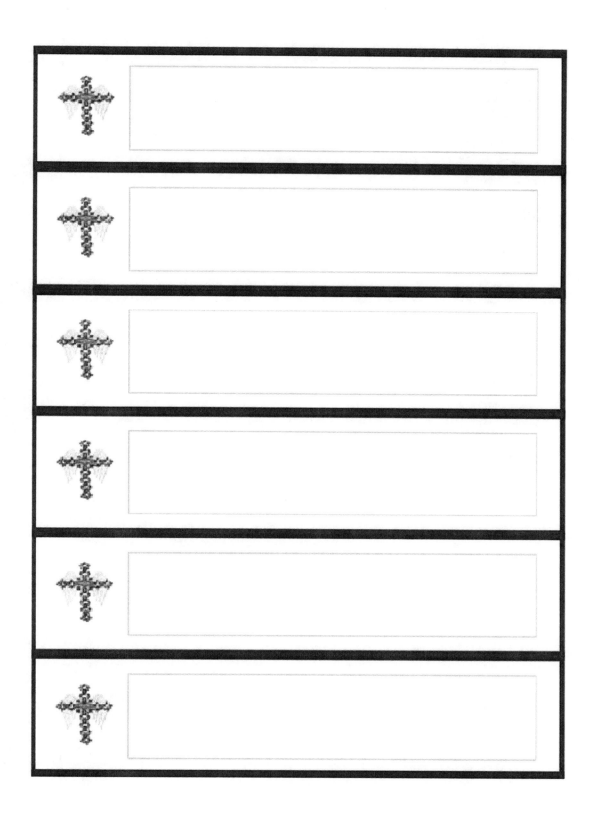

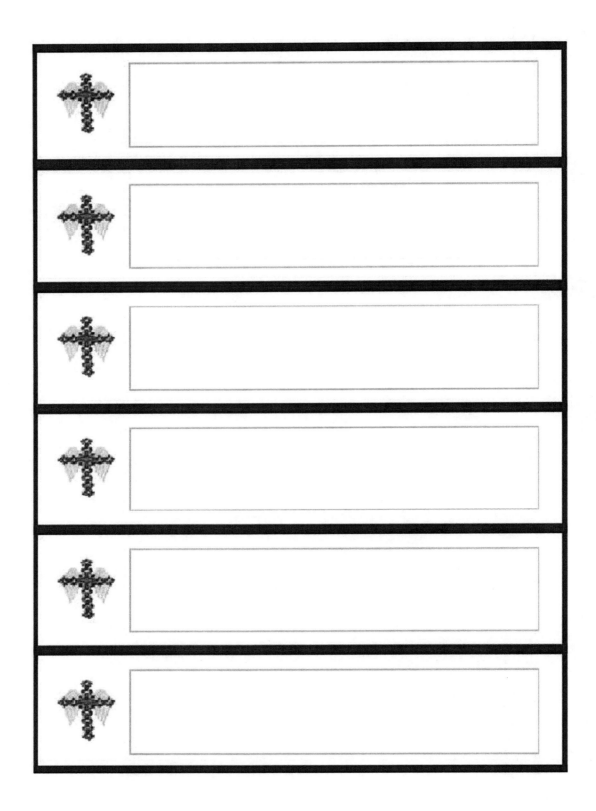

174

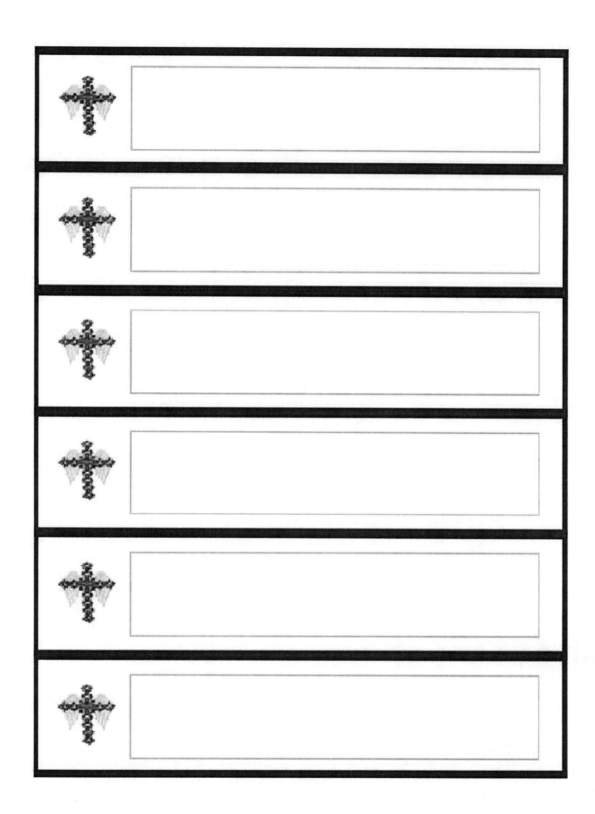

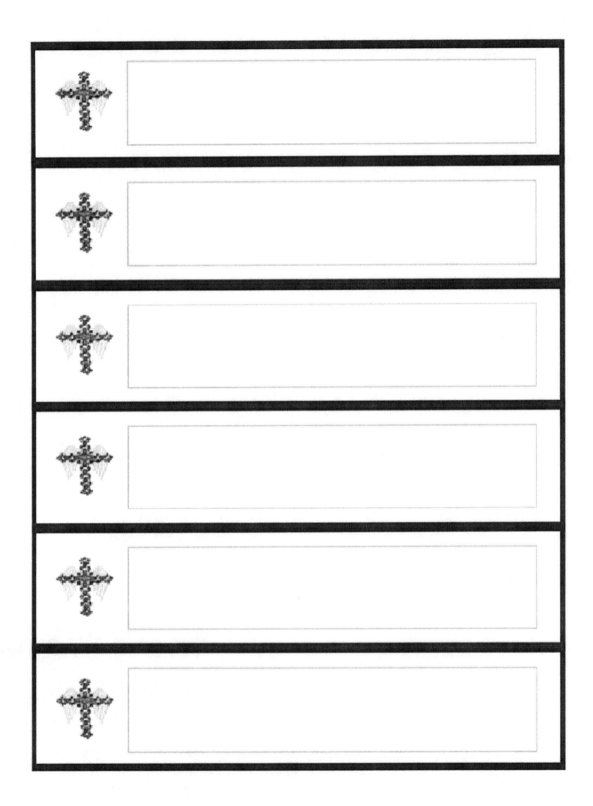

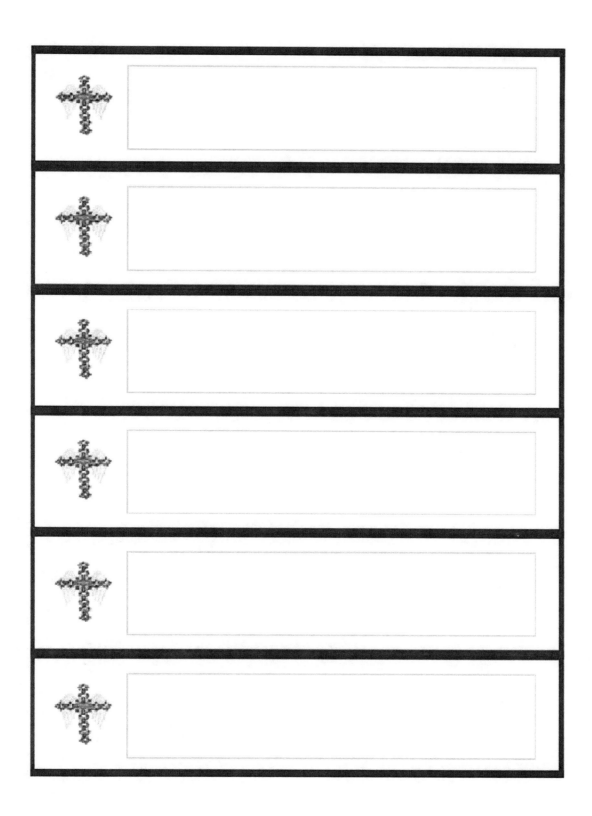

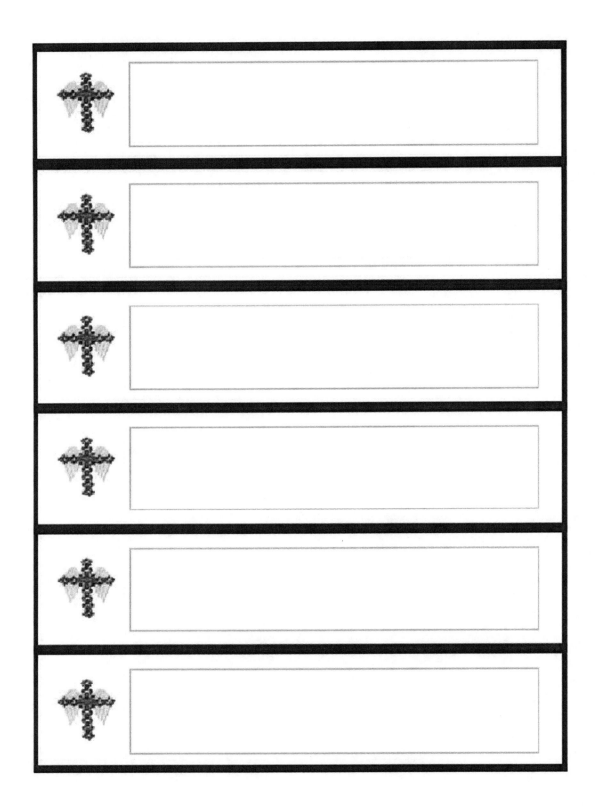

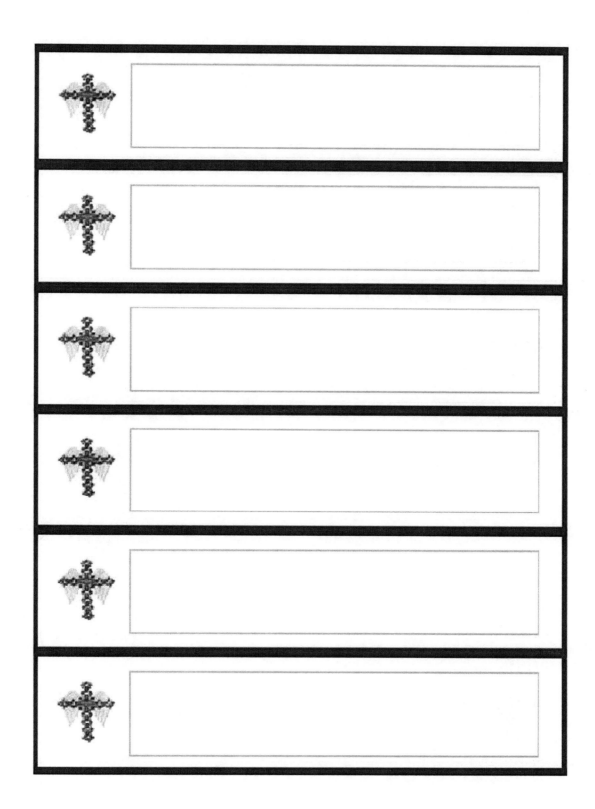

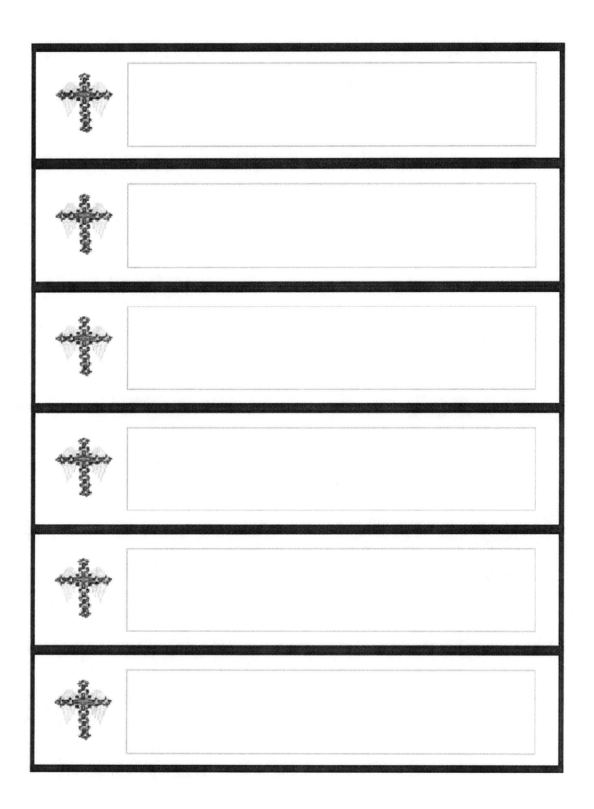

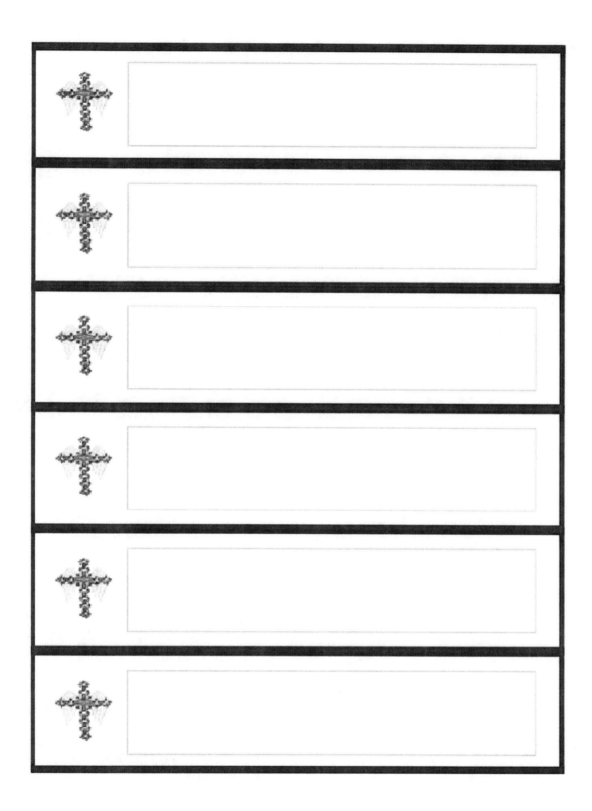

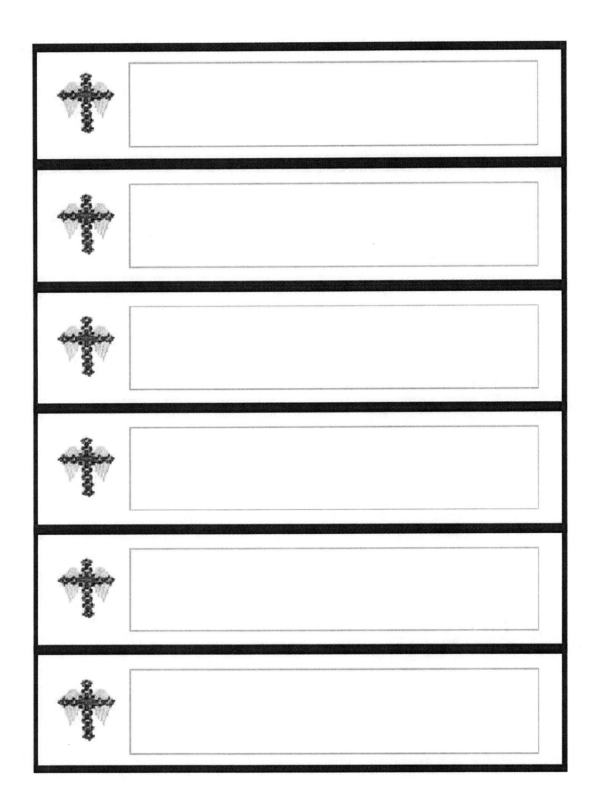

182

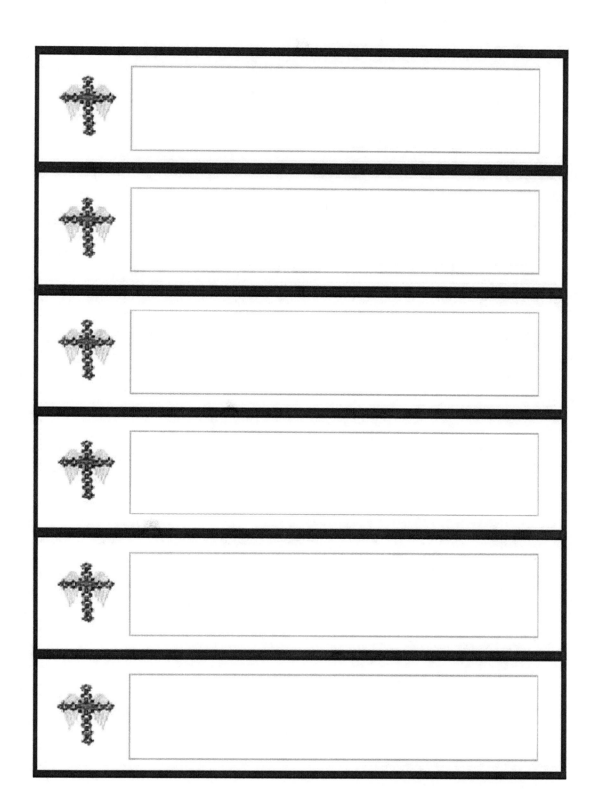

183

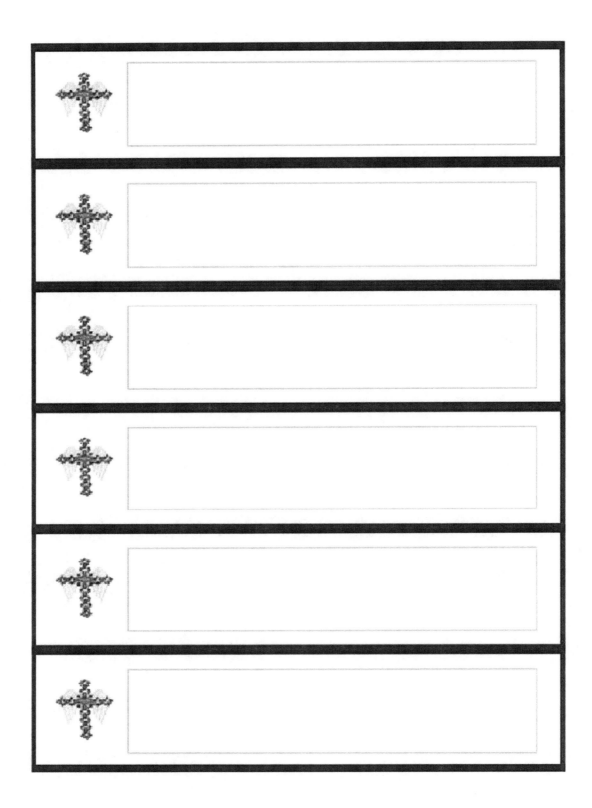

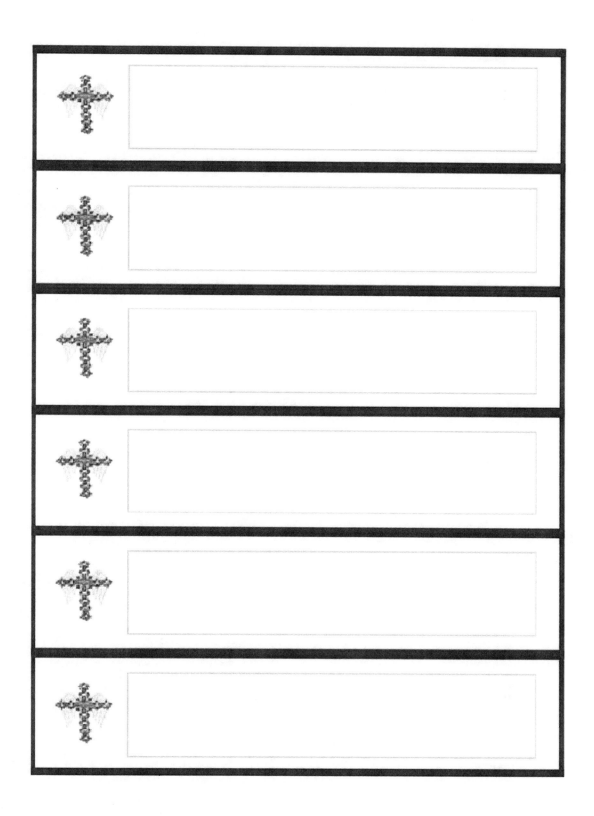

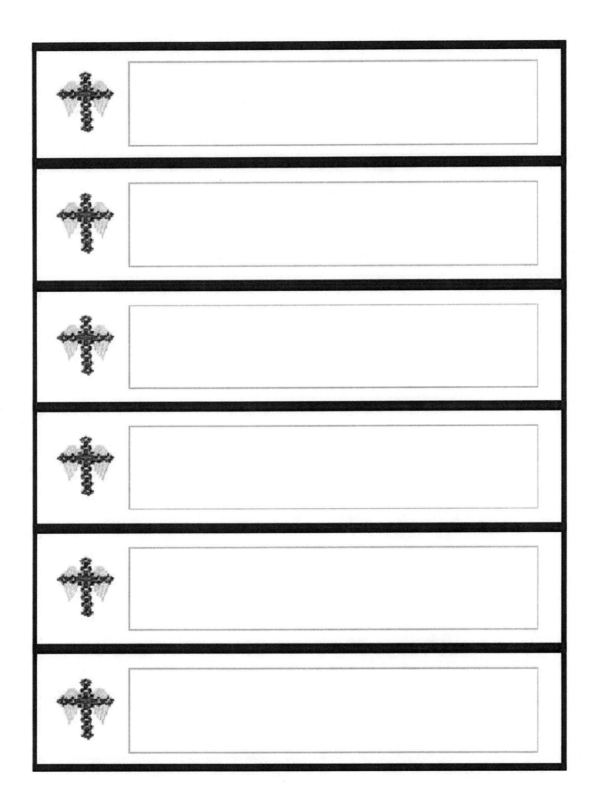

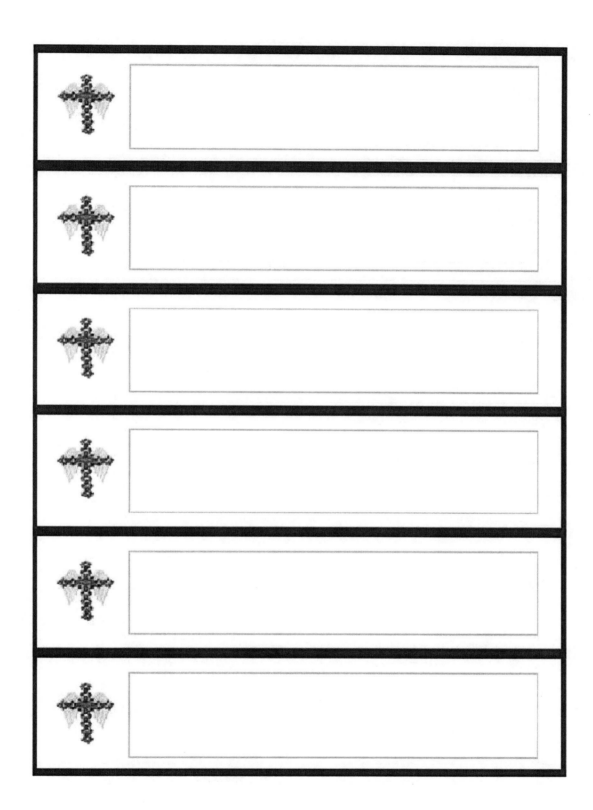

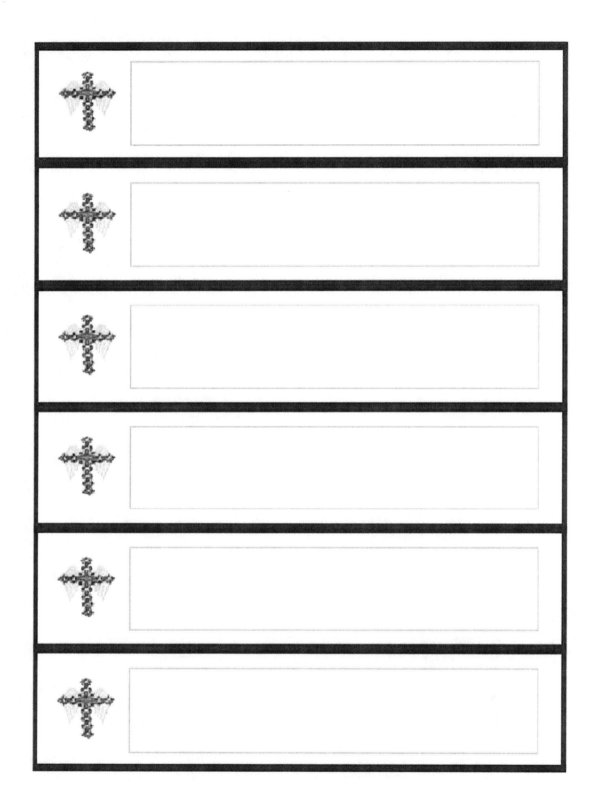

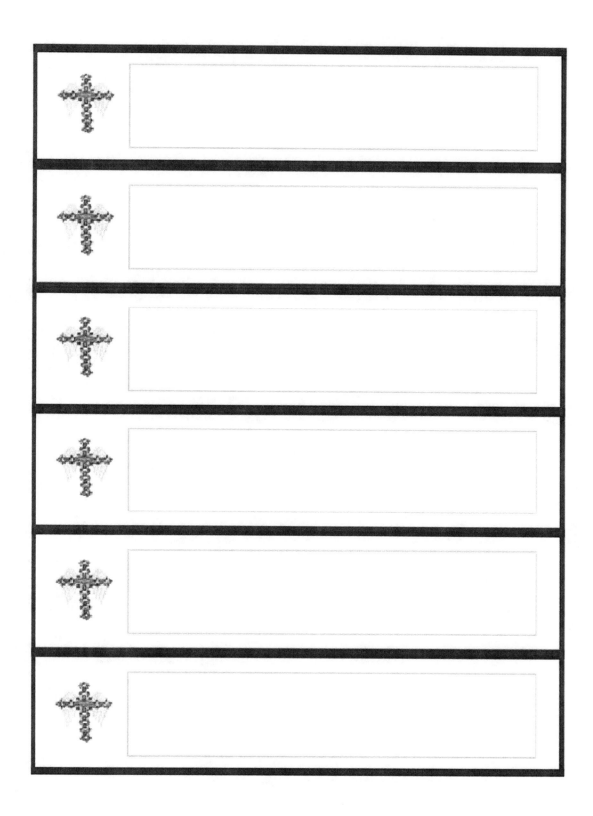

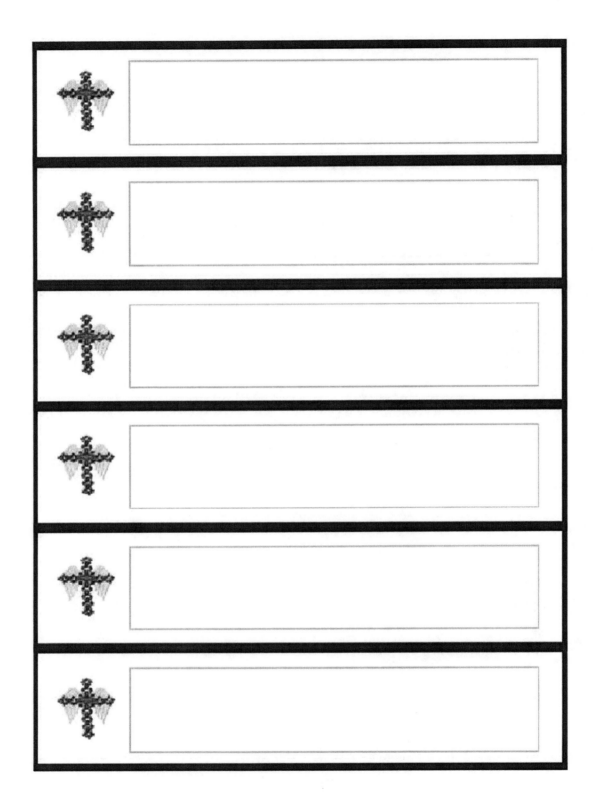

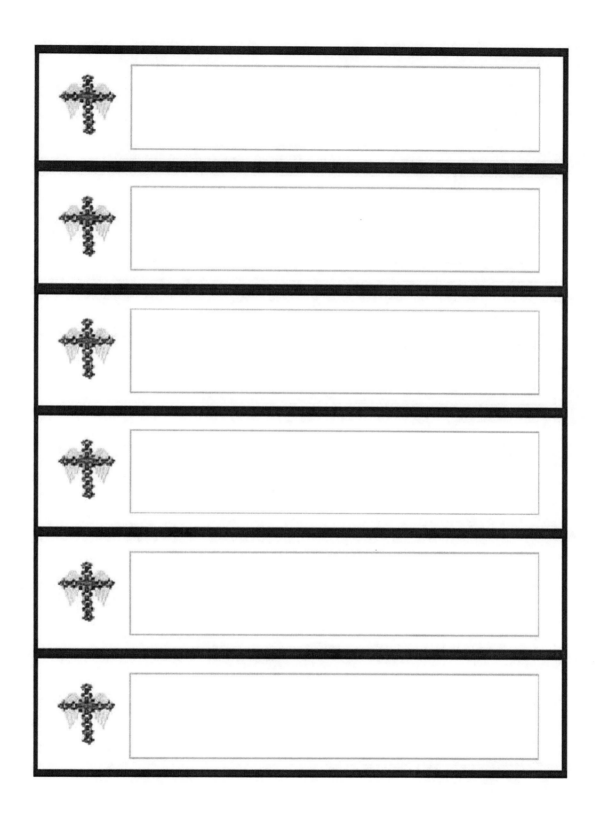

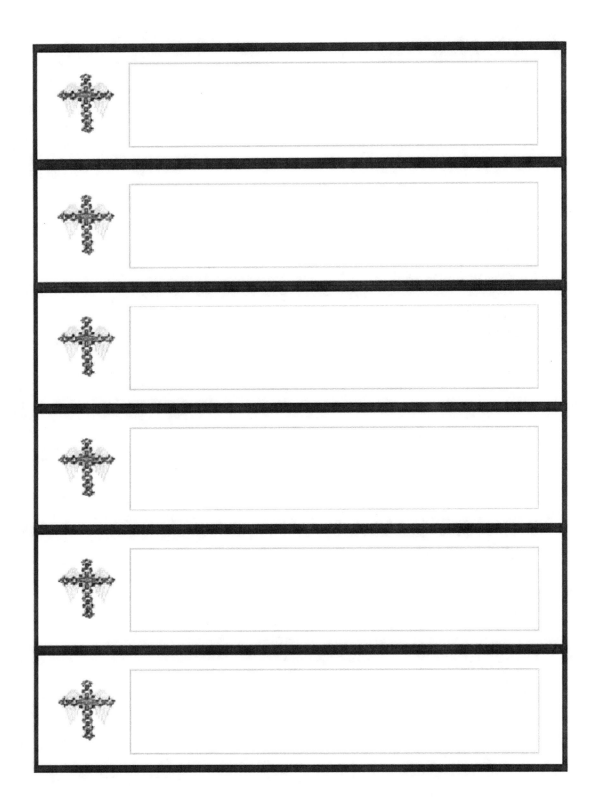

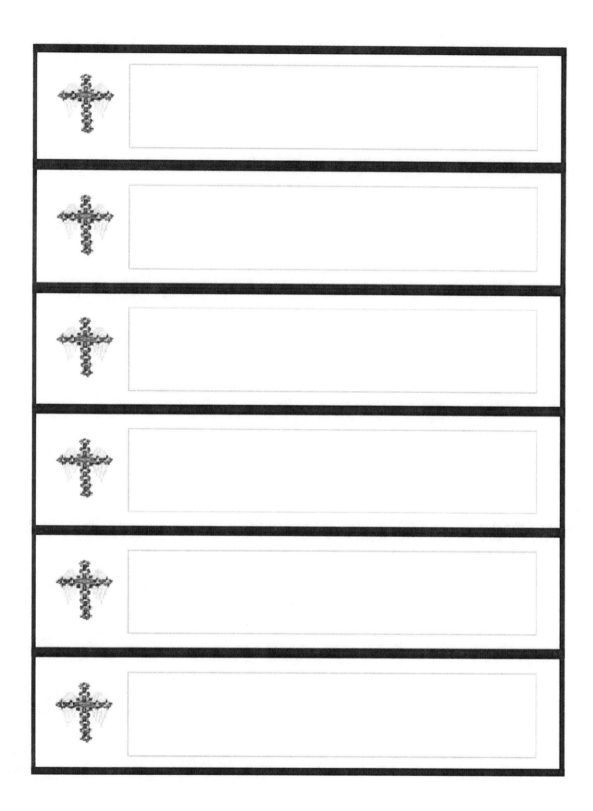

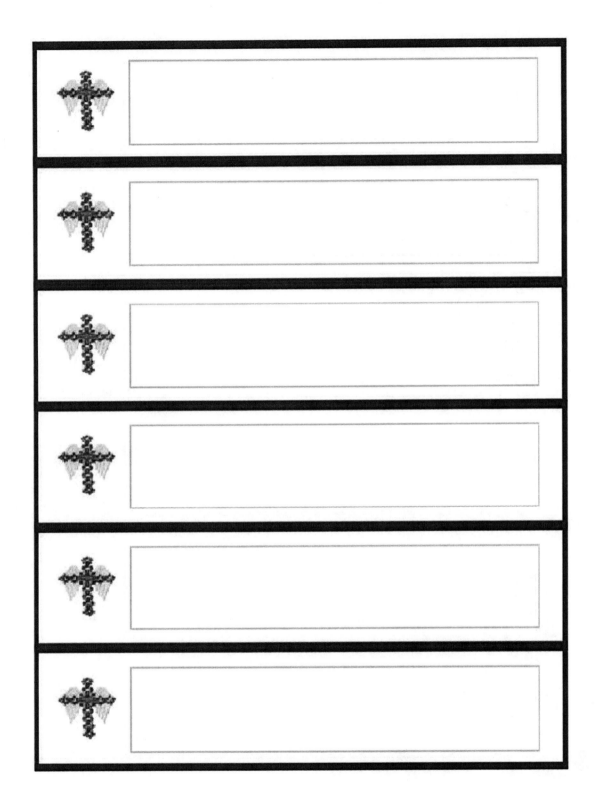

CHAPTER 14

TESTIMONIALS

Read The Results

Renee Arriaga, RN, MSN, FNP

"Life is so busy and hectic at times. During times of stress and disappointment in life, one forgets to 'walk in God's love.' Yvette helps us to remember to relax, take in a deep breath, and truly feel the unending love that Jesus Christ has for us."

Tamica L., Elementary School Teacher

"When I am feeling agitated, tense and stressed, after listening to the CD I feel relaxed, calm and peaceful. As a teacher, I find this Meditation & Prayer YDS CD a great way to start the school day, leaving the children calm, relaxed and receptive. The pace is great. I've tried four different meditation CDs, and this is the first one that didn't make me feel rushed."

Carlos Cepero, Loan Officer

"I felt drained after a stressful day at work. I was worried and anxious, and my breathing was shallow. After listening to the CD, I felt relaxed, revitalized, inspired, and hopeful that, no matter what comes my way, I will be able to get through it. The instructions were concise and easy to follow. I like being able to repeat tracks five through eight."

Rebecca Gomez, College Student

"My stresses have been coping with my Mom's passing away, the sexual abuse in my past, the loss of interest in my field of work, and the pressures from college, a car accident, and boyfriend drama. The meditation helped me to bring so many negative things to a halt. I was able to push out all of my worries. Anyone who is looking for a peaceful state of mind should use this meditation CD."

Richard, HPD Officer

"I suffered a hemorrhagic stroke. A few days later, my wife was driving me to the Texas Medical Center. She saw I was distraught and nervous. She remembered she had the *Meditation & Prayer YDS* CD in the car and quickly began to play it for me to do the exercises. After only a few minutes, calmness transcended my spirit. Suddenly, I felt peace and hope for my future. I was now ready for my angioplasty procedure with serenity and grace."

Houston Police Department

Tobie, Domestic Engineer of two boys

"When my children were born, my anxiety became more profound with fatigue and migraines. I started listening to the CD and found it very relaxing. It helped me change the way I think about myself, which caused me to release negative emotions and worry, reducing my anxiety, fatigue, and migraines. Every night I listen to the CD and the next day I am at ease and peace with more focus, because my mind is not filled with clutter and negative thoughts.

The added bonus was the calming effect on my two-and-a-half-year-old. He was not adjusting to his new toddler bed and kept getting up. I sat him next to me and we listened together. Before I knew it, he was sound asleep. I recommend Meditation & Prayer YDS to anyone."

Nina Georgalos, College Student

"This was my first time listening to a meditation CD, and I can honestly say I loved it. It was very relaxing and put me in a calm, peaceful state of mind. This would definitely be something I listen to before going to bed, to help end my day carefree and to begin the next day refreshed. Combining meditation with prayer is a successful method for me in relieving all my worries."

Claire Papin, Lighted Path & LIME/Sirius Satellite Radio

"Yvette Silva's Meditation & Prayer YDS CD is good for the mind and healing for the soul. It really gives me a boost of self-esteem when I am feeling low. I enjoy being able to skip around to the different tracks."

Steve Bouboudakis, Business Owner, Steve's Automotive; Uptown Collision Center

"Incredible! I have never meditated before in my life. The first-time experience was unbelievable. The instructions were very good and easy to follow. I like the scriptures at the end. Honestly, I felt very relaxed the next morning. Very highly recommended!"

Melissa Oquendo, College Student

"I stress about being a full-time mom, student, and worker. I wonder how I am going to have time for everything. I want to have time for my daughter and be a role model for her. I feel more calm and relaxed after listening to the CD. I feel free of stress, more positive toward myself and life, and that if I keep listening to this CD, the whole negativity toward life will disappear with faith."

T. Smith, Director of Employee Benefits

"I listened to the Meditation & Prayer YDS CD for the first time at the end of a very busy and stressful workday. I found myself almost immediately relaxing into bed. It's like your mind really does take a vacation. I could feel the peaceful and loving energy of the speaker coming through. I think this CD would benefit anyone who wants to calm their mind and develop their inner connection to their soul and to God."

Katrina Acevedo, College Student

"I miss my family in Puerto Rico, and I have no one to talk to. I stress about school starting and applying to the master's programs. Listening to this CD on meditation made me feel very relaxed and calm. I feel very refreshed and empowered."

T. Wright, Accountant

"I liked being able to stop and start the CD at my own pace. Having only tried meditation once, I found it easy to relax and truly meditate. I believe this CD would be very useful for those individuals in a high-stress profession."

Paul Weisser, PhD, UC Berkeley—
Editor, Writer, Desktop Publisher

"I have worked with Yvette editing the journal and workbook of Meditation & Prayer YDS, (MP YDS) I am of Eastern faith, if you will, but I really enjoyed the MP YDS Christian-based program. I believe it will be helpful to those who want to learn to meditate, and will bring a little peace in a hectic life. I would recommend this to teachers and parents with troubled or challenging children, or those needing to improve self-esteem.

I was questioning and drilling Yvette about her past and I realized the past was not easy for her to speak about during our editing sessions. I truly believe and know that what she has endured and survived makes her exceedingly qualified to teach this program she has written. I am astounded at her strength to persevere and not give up, and at her compassion to help others get through their trials and tribulations.

Yvette gives easy step-by-step direction that is really for all faiths."

CHAPTER 15

AGREEMENT FORMS

Share Your Story

AGREEMENT FORMS

Share Your Story

This journey of writing the *Meditation & Prayer YDS LLC* program has been the hardest thing I have ever gone through. Dear Reader, it was easy keeping those negative emotions to myself while keeping my secrets tucked away in my heart for so long that it was difficult to let everything go and let you in. I always knew that I was safe behind my wall, because that's what I was accustomed to. I am now transparent to you in the hope that you will let your pain out of your heart, let God in, and find happiness, as I have.

If you feel that you are in a safe place and can share your story with me, I will be honored! If you feel comfortable enough to allow me to share your letter, photo, or video diary with others on my website www.mpyds.com, or on Facebook: Meditation & Prayer YDS, or in a documentary, I would be even more honored.

Complete the agreement form below, tell your story on the back, tear out the page, and mail it to the postal address below, or scan the page and email it to SilvaUniverse@yahoo.com. Put "Testimonial" in the subject line. If you would prefer to only state how the Meditation & Prayer YDS program helped you, I will be blessed.

Your story just may help or inspire someone else in a similar situation as yours.

Postal Address:

Meditation & Prayer YDS LLC
Yvette Silva
P.O. Box 800574
Houston, TX 77280

Prayer Is Speaking to God. Meditation Is Listening to God.™

AGREEMENT FORM

Print below and return this completed form to the address listed below.

I, _____, hereby authorize Meditation & Prayer YDS LLC (hereinafter YDS LLC) to use any personal information I have submitted to YDS LLC, as well as any photographs, likenesses, entries, emails, or associated materials, including but not limited to use in advertisements, websites, CDs, brochures, documentaries, workbooks, books, health fairs, publications, television programs, internet sites, and/or seminar media, without acknowledgment or fees to me. I understand that these materials may be edited and become the property of YDS LLC.

I fully understand that this is a Christian-based program. _____ Initials

_____   _____
           Signature   Date

<u>Initial your preferences on the appropriate lines below:</u>

Use First Name only   Yes _____   No _____

Use First Initial Last Name   Yes _____   No _____

Use First Name Last Initial   Yes _____   No _____

Use Full Name   Yes _____   No _____

Use School Name   Yes _____   No _____

Use Church Name   Yes _____   No _____

Use Employment Position/Title Yes _____   No _____

(No Company Names)

Full Name: _____

Address: _____   City/Zip _____

Home phone #: _____   Cell phone #: _____

Email: _____

Employment Position: _____

Name of Church: _____

Name of School: _____

TESTIMONIAL

_____

_____

_____

_____

_____

_____

_____

_____

_____

_____

_____

_____

_____

_____

_____

_____

_____

_____

_____

_____

_____

_____

_____

Signature _____

I release all statements within to Meditation & Prayer YDS LLC to use for any purpose.

CPSIA information can be obtained at www.ICGtesting.com
Printed in the USA
LVOW09s0101181013

357443LV00001B/1/P